Single Wisdom

Empowering Singles, Divorcees,
Widows & Widowers for Living...
a Purposeful Life of Integrity and Learning
the Art of Establishing Healthy Romantic
and Marital Relationships

Paris M. Finner-Williams, Ph.D., L.P., Esq.

and

Robert D. Williams, LMSW, ACSW, DCSW, LMFT, CAC-I

Published by RP Publishing   (313) 537-1000

Cover artwork by Alva McNeal

Book artwork by Debra Terrell

Scripture quotations marked (NLT) are taken from the Holy Bible, New Living Translation, copyright © 1996. Used by permission of Tyndale House Publishers, Inc., Wheaton, Illinois 60189. All rights reserved.

Scripture quotations marked (KJV) are from the King James Version of the Bible.

Scripture quotations marked (KJV Amplified) are from the King James Amplified Version of the Bible.

Portions of this book are taken from *Marital Secrets: Dating, Lies, Communication and Sex*, by Paris M. Finner-Williams and Robert D. Williams.

ISBN No.: 0-9707527-1-7

Printed in the United States of America

Library of Congress Cataloging-in-Publication Data

Finner-Williams, Paris M. (Paris Michele), 1951-
Single wisdom : empowering singles, divorcees, widows &
widowers for living— a purposeful life of integrity and learning the
art of establishing healthy romantic and marital relationships / Paris
M. Finner-Williams and Robert D. Williams.
p. cm.
Includes bibliographical references and index.
ISBN 0-9707527-1-7
1. Single people—Psychology. 2. Single people—Religious life. 3.
Mate selection—Religious aspects—Christianity. 4. Man-woman
relationships—Religious aspects—Christianity. I. Williams, Robert
D. (Robert Dee), 1948- II. Title.
HQ800.F53 2005
248.8'4—dc22
2005005982

This book is dedicated to the awesome, beautiful and holy men and women of God that we know who are divorced, widowed, or never married. We honor, love and respect each and every one of you.

Contents

About the Authors

Dr. Attorney Paris Michele Finner-Williams has been a professional mental health pioneer since 1972 and she is a:

- Fully Licensed Clinical Psychologist
- Forensic Examiner Diplomat
- Certified Rehabilitation Counselor
- Certified Christian Mediator
- Certified Trauma Services Specialist
- Certified Christian Counselor
- Licensed Attorney and Counselor at Law
- Author, Trainer and Conference Speaker

Finner-Williams is the founder and chief executive officer of the Detroit-based Finner-Williams and Associates Psychological Services, created in 1979, and the legal professional association of Paris M. Finner-Williams, Esq., P.C., created in 1991. She was born and raised in Detroit and holds a Bachelor of Arts degree in psychology from the University of Detroit, a Master of Education degree in educational psychology from Wayne State University, a Doctor of Philosophy degree in psychological counseling from the University of Michigan, and a Juris Doctorate from the Detroit College of Law, which is now a department at Michigan State University.

A popular guest on radio and television, Finner-Williams addresses male-female relationships and motivational issues. She is an author of numerous publications and articles and is often quoted as a relationship expert in popular magazines such as *Ebony* and *Jet*. Her counseling and legal services include these issues as well as forensic psychology, rehabilitation, divorce law, family law and probate matters. An advocate of church-based Christian counseling, she is a founder and the first chairperson of the Black African-American Christian Counselors Division of the American Association of Christian Counselors.

Finner-Williams provides free monthly training services to the local Christian Counselors through her Finner-Williams Christian Counseling Ministry, a not-for-profit corporation.

Formerly a mental health administrator, Finner-Williams has an extensive history of program development and management. She provides consultation and training to public and private agencies and organizations in the areas of group dynamics, forensic psychology, client assessment, and mental health treatment. She is a member in or officer of numerous professional organizations and has received local and national recognition for her contributions and leadership in the mental health field. Finner-Williams has volunteered time as the legal consultant for the International Association of Black Psychologists since 1989, has received their Service Award on several occasions and was granted the 2006 Distinguished Psychologist of the Year Award. Her husband, Robert D. Williams, and she work together in their private practice to preserve families and couples and help individuals. They are the co-authors of *Marital Secrets*: *Dating, Lies, Communication and Sex* (2001)*, Single Wisdom* (2005), and *How To Develop A Church-Based Christian Counseling Ministry* (2006), which are available anywhere books are sold and through their own publishing company, RP Publishing.

Mr. Robert Dee Williams is an author of numerous publications and articles, and the co-author of *Marital Secrets: Dating, Lies, Communication and Sex* (2001), *Single Wisdom* (2005), and *How To Develop A Church-Based Christian Counseling Ministry* (2006), along with his wife Dr. Atty. Paris M. Finner-Williams. He is a nationwide radio personality, TV guest, and trainer on topics pertaining to group work; treatment of the chronically mentally ill; treatment of African-American males; romantic relationships, male-female relationship issues; marriage and family; child, adolescent and teen problems; self-esteem; motivation; attitude; violence in the workplace; policies and procedures; and clinical practice. He has a Master of Arts degree in social work, and is a member of the Academy of Certified Social Workers, a Licensed Marriage and Family Therapist, and a Diplomat in Clinical Social Work. Robert is also a Certified Forensic Addiction Examiner and Certified Addiction Counselor. He has been a Senior Team Leader and Manager at local Community Mental Health Corporations and residential treatment programs for adjudicated youth for several decades, and the Executive Director of the Finner-Williams and Associates Psychological Services since 1988.

Mr. Williams has been in clinical practice and mental health administration since 1973. He is a member of the National Association of Black Social Workers, National Association of Social Workers, and Association for the Advancement of Social Work with Groups since 1973. He has served on the Board of Directors of these professional groups and served as President of the University of Michigan School of Social Workers Alumni Board of Advisors.

Preface

When people think about relationships, they think: love, loneliness, heartache, romance, and betrayal. They rarely, however, think: *wisdom.*

Wisdom. The mere mention of the word evokes cold, emotionless, philosophical conjecture—which couldn't be farther from the truth. In a society that has been turned upside-down, we can no longer ignore the need to include wisdom in our conversations about relationships and life.

We cringe at this misunderstood word, because we are relational beings and think our ideas and behavior should be driven primarily by emotion. How many times have we been encouraged to follow how we *felt* when it may have been more beneficial to consider what the *wisest* choice would be? Being emotional is not wrong, but how do we go about including wisdom in our decision making process and how will it in turn help?

In the epistle of James, we learn how our desire can lead and entice us into making unwise decisions that will ultimately lead to an undesired end (James 1:14ff). The term that is used for lust or desire is *epithumias*, which is strongly rooted in our passion. James's warning is given to move us from emotionally-based decision-making to a process that incorporates God's direction. Likewise, the biblical collection of Proverbs is packed with admonitions that advocate the uncompromising and essential need for personal wisdom. One of these wise sayings implores:

> My child, if you accept my words and treasure up
> my commandments within you, making your ear
> attentive to wisdom and inclining your heart to

understanding; if you indeed cry out for insight, and
raise your voice for understanding; if you seek it
like silver, and search for it as for hidden treasures
then you will understand the fear of the LORD and
find the knowledge of God. For the LORD gives
wisdom; from his mouth come knowledge and
understanding (Proverbs 2:1, NRSV).

As we consider wisdom, we must also remember that there are
two kinds. There is the *world's wisdom* (*Cf.* 1 Corinthians 1:20,
3:19), which often leads to the ruin of many lives and relationships.
And there is *divine wisdom*—that is, wisdom that comes from God.
Those of us who face life's complex issues must consider *chacmah*,
the Hebrew term that describes wisdom. *Chacmah* encompasses
multiple concepts: skill and experience, understanding how to
handle situations, and making effectual and prudent decisions. We
receive this kind of wisdom not by simply attending a course in
psychology or philosophy, however beneficial those may be, but
rather by seeking a relationship with God through his son Jesus.

James's epistle states, "If any of you is lacking in wisdom, ask
God, who gives to all generously and ungrudgingly, and it will
be given you" (James 1:5, NRSV). Here the Greek term *sophia*
implies a similar sense as its Hebrew counterpart *chacmah*. The use
of godly wisdom provides an opportunity to objectively evaluate
ourselves and the situations in which we find ourselves. We then
have a basis to make decisions based on divine wisdom versus
what is frankly our own subjective concoction of what we think
may be good for us.

The call to wisdom has been sounded. If we are to turn the
ship of broken relationships and unhealthy lifestyles around it
must begin with a commitment to appropriating divine wisdom.
Helpful ideas abound, but we still must be conscious that the
majority of any society's set of morals, values, and customs are a
product of a pluralistic and accommodating environment—often
too accommodating for Christians to emulate without evaluating in
the light of God's Word. If we trust too much in what we see at the

movies, or the latest talk show, we may jeopardize our chances for having a viable and enjoyable relationship, not only with others, but more importantly with God.

Every delicate situation that arises from being single beckons to us: "Trust in the LORD with all your heart, and do not rely on your own insight" (Proverbs 3:5, NRSV). Let *Single Wisdom* provide you with wise answers and counsel for your most important decisions and choices.

Rodney A. Caruthers, II., M. Div.
Spring Arbor University

Foreword

When the Authors sent me the galleys to write the foreword, I rejoiced that this single volume contained so much wisdom for living life abundantly in whatever state you find yourself whether, single or married. There are numerous books written on relationships and how they evolve but this text goes beyond just more information and provides insight and inspiration that will lead to revelation on how to enrich your single life and enhance your marital life. Professionals in the field of mental health (psychologist, counselors, clinical social workers, etc.) as well as clergy and university professors will find this text a very relevant and practical resource.

As a colleague, having also written books on relationships, I can appreciate the depth of their research, the candor of their transparency and the extent of their accomplishment. Robert and Paris have written a timeless resource that will be instrumental in years to come. As co-laborers in the Kingdom, Robert and Paris have poured themselves out to make a difference in the lives of others. Praise God that even prior to meeting, they cared enough about themselves to spend time in personal development instead of searching for someone else to make them whole. Having heard their stories and now witnessed the reality of their love one for another, I know that they have a wealth of information to share about the "how to's" of singleness and married life.

It's not often that you find a book that is Biblical, clinical, legal and humorous. They have a way of engaging you in the lives of the characters throughout the book that will help you to stop crying about where you are and learn to embrace the significance of your present state. Every reader will find something of value in this book.

It is critical in every relationship to seek WISDOM. Enjoy this meaningful journey of self discovery as you gain wisdom that will transform your life.

> Dr. Sabrina D. Black, International Speaker,
> Counselor and co-Author of "Prone To Wander,"
> "HELP! for Your Leadership," "Counseling in the
> African American Community" and "Can Two Walk
> Together: Spiritual Encouragement for Unequally
> Yoked Marriages"
> President, National Biblical Counselors Association
> Chairperson, Black African American Christian
> Counselors

Acknowledgments

Thank you, God, for giving us favor and the presence of the Holy Spirit that has guided us and made possible the birth and completion of this project. To God be the glory!

There are family members who have loved us and nourished our spirits. We want to express our appreciation to Dr. Gerald B. McAdoo, Mrs. Bernice McAdoo, VerShaun Sherice Finner, MSW, Mr. Gerald and Mrs. Angela McAdoo, and Dr. Jernice L. McAdoo, Thelma Jean Finner, RN, BSN, MS, Cheryl Bell, Esq. and Dr. N. Thomas Howard. We want to thank Curtis Williams, Lula Mae Williams, Rev. and Mrs. Jimmy T. Wafer and Ms. Avalyn Smith and a host of other brothers, sisters, cousins, aunts and uncles. There are extended family members who have embraced us and encouraged us: Patricia Soares; Gloria A. Truss, Esq.; Chuck and Paulette Means; Rev. Estella Brown; Dr. William Revely, Jr.; Dr. Linda Wharton Boyd; our church family; and the several pastors and ministers who have so graciously allowed us to work with their single members, marital couples and with their marital couples ministries.

We are appreciative of those who have prayed and stood in the gap for us and served as a constant source of support: David and Kim Peeples; Dr. Larry Richardson; Ms. Rose Chaney; Mrs. Caroline Pearson; Rev. George Hawkins; Evangelist De'Borah Donald; and Ms. Bernice Laster.

We want to thank those who have served as our technical and literary experts: Rebecca Florence Osaigbovo; Diane Proctor Reeder; Pam Perry; Mrs. Clementine Strong; Doni Owens; Rev. Rodney Caruthers, II; Tracie Lynn Hicks; Gail Elizabeth Hicks; and Tiffany Elizabeth Smith, Alva McNeal and Debra Ann Terrell.

We are grateful to God for blessing our lives with these and so many other beautiful people.

Introduction

In our clinical practice, and in our private lives, we have been blessed to meet and come to know wonderful and good hearted persons who have never married, who are divorced or who are now widowed. It has often troubled our hearts to witness how they approach living, dating and marriage, knowing that with a few words of wisdom they could enhance the quality of their singleness and enjoy their journey to whatever destination God has designed for them.

If you're a divorcee, we'd like to show you how to successfully recover from divorce and teach you effective healing techniques. If you're a widow or widower, we'd like to show you how to craft new wineskins for your new life—and give you permission to enjoy the sweet fragrance of your past memories. If you've never been married, we'd like to show you how to break strongholds, yokes and generational curses so you can be more attractive romantically and move toward spiritual wholeness. In short, if you're single, it is our wish to share with you the art of transforming your single life into joy and, if you so choose, establish healthy romantic and marital relationships that will honor our Lord and Savior Jesus Christ.

The goal of this book is to share more than sixty years of combined therapeutic and legal experience by two people who have been married to each other for more than sixteen years, and counseled even longer. Come and learn to travel the singleness road in a way that will allow stretch and grow you in your walk of faith. Come and learn the lessons we have learned from others and from ourselves. We are committed to helping you transform your life through self-knowledge and self-empowerment.

In no way is this book intended to serve as a substitute for the Holy Bible or for seeking and receiving counseling or therapy from a qualified mental health professional or Christian counselor. We recommend that you study the Word of God and seek such professional services if your situation so indicates.

This book explores the three different groups of singles and studies what we have learned from others. We examine how to obliterate barriers and strongholds formed by the needs of the flesh so that single men and women can have satisfying romantic relationships. We provide solutions, techniques and approaches that are practical and have proven effective for enhancing romantic relationships among single individuals. We hope this book will be a blessing to you and enhance your ability to gain the God-given power, internal light of peace and joy that God intends for your life.

This is a self-help book for big boys and girls who are mature enough and strong enough to face, discuss and resolve those intense and serious issues and barriers between men and women in romantic relationships.

So come and journey with Nia, Pace and Carol, and learn what they can do to make their lives better. We hope you are enlightened by—and enjoy—the ride!

Chapter One

The Journey of Life

The Profile of Nia

Nia was a child born to an unwed mother—one who was disabled with anger, shame, fear and overwhelming responsibility for the life she carried in her belly. Nia's mother was angry at Nia's daddy, who made it very clear from the beginning that he didn't want anything else to do with Nia or her mother. She was angry with herself for believing the words of love spoken to her by Nia's father. She was ashamed that she allowed one night of unprotected lust to result in an unplanned and unwanted pregnancy. She was afraid that she would not be a proper mother to this vulnerable and innocent child.

But despite all the negative emotions and thoughts, Nia's mother pressed her way to the nearest public telephone, called her mother's house, and told the truth. She knew she would have to confess her sin, bury her pride, and submit herself to her elders. Only then could Nia's mother's next choices be wise, clear and rational. Only then would she have a fighting chance of surviving the consequences of her one unwise night.

Nia's mother searched in her cluttered purse for coins, prayed to God for strength, composed herself, and dialed the telephone number that had not changed in fifty years, the telephone number that had always connected her to a valuable storehouse of love and armor-bearers. That nightmarish day in June was warm, but she felt cold from the inside out in that doctor's office lobby. "Mama, I have something to tell you," she said, "and I need you to listen and not go off on me, OK? The doctor said I'm three months pregnant, and it's Ray's baby. Mama, I'm sorry—I messed up. What should I do?"

That call sent shivers through Nia's mother's mother, too. "Lord have mercy! Lord give me strength. Yes, baby I've been dreaming about fish all month—I already thought so. The Lord will provide.

You know I taught you better than this! This did not have to happen! Your life is about to change. Lord have mercy! Where are you now? Do you need me to send your brother to get you?"

"No mama—I can get the bus back home. I need to think things over."

"Baby, don't do anything stupid. Just get home safely and then we'll decide what we will do."

"Yes, ma'am. I love you."

"I love you too, baby. I'll see you when you get home."

Nia's widowed grandmother finally had the attention of Nia's mother. In that day, abortion was not a popular option in Christian families. So in mid-March of the next year Nia was born, weighing four pounds fourteen ounces and with a full, intact membranous sheet over her face, called a "veil" in the African American community.

Nia grew up in two places: the sterile house created by her lonely twenty-nine-year-old mother who often drank away her sadness; and four blocks away at the warm nourishing feet of her deeply spiritual maternal grandmother. Her six uncles, five aunts, a host of cousins, relatives, friends, neighbors, and church family formed the nourishing village that molded Nia's values and morals and provided for her every need.

From her grandmother, Nia learned how to develop a daily prayer life, how to discern God's will for her life and how to daily walk with our Lord and Savior Jesus Christ.

From her aunts she learned about business, persistence, effective problem resolution skills, the value of humor, the essence of family life, important daily living skills, and how to command respect. These ladies of character conveyed to her a sense of style, self-pride and true Christian faith and hope.

From her mother Nia learned about sexuality and romance, and the value of solitude, sacrifice, forgiveness, and tolerance.

From her cousins Nia learned the value of faithfulness, unconditional love, support, encouragement and comradeship.

Nia learned something else, too—'lessons' that were not quite as positive—from her biological father. From him, Nia learned lessons embedded in the painful cycle of rejection and alienation. Nia felt, almost in a physical way, the absence of her father. The empty space where her father should have been was filled with want, emptiness, abandonment, and hopelessness. The unfortunate result? Attraction to unhealthy relations and attachment to superficial admirers—poor substitutes for her father, but quite enough for a girl whose father decided not to be there.

Fortunately Nia's uncles stood in that gap and taught Nia lessons of contentment, peace, pride, and humility. Proven men of integrity, accountability, professional purpose and Christian male responsibility, her uncles did the best they could. It was not enough, however, to completely make up for 'daddy hunger,' which became even more acute when Nia reached twelve years of age.

She managed to conspire with one of her uncles to meet her father for the first time in June. Nia was filled with excitement and anticipation as she entered her father's barber shop on that warm Saturday afternoon. Her blue lace Sunday church dress was pressed and her black patent leather shoes were polished. Her uncle was well groomed in his suit and tie. After all, they both had conspired to lie to Nia's grandmother, telling her they were to enjoy a lunch date in celebration of Nia's straight "A" card marking. Grandma believed it. She died four years later without learning the truth.

The special moment arrived and Nia's uncle made the introductions: "Ray—this is your daughter Nia. Nia, this is your father." Out of the awkward silence Nia recalls vividly that her father boastfully and arrogantly responded with "It's about time you came to see me."

Her father's cold, heartless response transformed Nia before her uncle's eyes. He saw in her eyes a look that he did not recognize—a look that signaled a changed disposition, an eerie reflection of her mother. In that moment, Nia lost her innocence.

Nia's next visit with her father was approximately ten years later in the funeral home sanctuary as he lay in the casket. For Nia, to look upon his face in the casket was to glimpse of her own final visitation. She closed the parlor room doors, sat on the front bench and made peace with her earthly father. The tears flowed, the anger abated and there was a sense of closure and resolution, a sense of peace that flows from total acceptance of reality. Nia felt peace with the death of her dream to have a meaningful relationship with her biological father. It was well with her soul, but the damage from the paternal gap lingered on.

One year later, when Nia's mother died, Nia realized that she had had that same dream—to have a meaning relationship with Ray, the father of her only child. How sad that two women held on to the Willie dream for nearly twenty-five years without Ray having an inkling of their suffering anguish.

At the age of twelve, before the painful incident with her aborted reconciliation with her father, before her eyes lost their innocence, Nia accepted the Lord Jesus Christ as her Savior. During the next ten years of alienation from her absent father Nia fell deeply into the resulting pain and destruction. Like her mother, there was a gross disconnect between the love and good lessons learned from her family and the poor self-image, poor self-esteem, lack of self-confidence and unhealthy romantic choices that she made. Despite her family's best efforts, the paternal gap resulted in her continuing to feel rejected, inadequate, unacceptable, and unloved by good men. She grew up trying to fill the gap by over indulging in food, sex, and education.

The warm food brought acceptance and an inner physical and emotional comfort that she did not receive from males. Unfortunately, the food addiction lead to obesity, three life-threatening medical conditions, and furthered her poor self-image and poor self-esteem. The momentary gratification of sex and pretend romance with single and married men led to unexpected pregnancies, multiple abortions, and the rekindling of those negative feelings Nia learned from her father's absence. The sexual encounters and unhealthy toxic relationships, as before, left her feeling rejected, alone, abandoned, hopeless and guilty. Nia would buy her male friends gifts and presents, but their commitment and love did not follow Nia's generous giving. Her holidays were just as lonely. Her dreams remained foggy. Her spirit felt an emptiness and she grew to be fearful, self-protective, oversensitive, unforgiving, suspicious and harsh. But the next man always managed to pierce the shield—at least for a while.

Having failed in love, Nia learned to succeed in education. She wanted to marry, but having no 'worthy' candidates, she pursued multiple degrees, licenses and certifications. Her education and professional success was one means to fill her paternal gap. There was no alienation when it came to education—Nia could go to college with no fear of rejection and at the same time enhance her knowledge, skills and abilities. Each graduation and degree boosted Nia's self-esteem and confidence. The gratification that Nia received from her demanding professional work filled the gap in Nia's life better than her prior indulgences with food and sex. So instead of becoming a wife and mother, Nia became a competent, well-liked and respected professional woman.

But all was not well. Nia was a target for envy and jealousy by colleagues and friends alike, and that surprised her. They didn't know her personal struggle for sanity and peace. How could they know what it was really like, what it had really been like?

That was the point. They couldn't know. Nia kept a veil over her history and her feelings. Her public image was good. No one knew the secret pain she carried.

Nia was faithful to God but slow to learn her purpose in life, how to discern God's will for her life, and how to daily walk in her faith. So Nia was highly productive during the week but would fall into the septic tank of depression at the close of work each day and even deeper each Friday. Nia's face flooded with tears from her employer's parking lot and continued during her journey home. She repeatedly circled the block until she gained composure enough to enter the family home without being interrogated about her tears. The damaging paternal gap was still felt.

Nia grew frustrated with her life. She was productive but miserable. She was saved by God but felt hopeless and helpless. She was lonely and grew suspicious of the motives of men. She grew older, impatient and uncertain whether God was going to provide her a husband. The fear of growing old alone was a morning and evening image that zapped her joy. Nia resented being told to obey the biblical scriptures of a God who appeared not to care about her suffering and her need for companionship, security and human touch. It was indeed difficult to worship and praise the Lord and fully comply with the Holy Scriptures while living a single Christian life.

Are you on the church pew with Nia?

The Profile of Pace   Nia

Pace was conflicted and convinced by Paul's belief that "if they cannot contain, let them marry: for it is better to marry than to burn" (I. Corinthians 7:9). Pace was a twenty-four-year-old "near virgin," (meaning he had some intense physical romantic contact with women, but had never actually had intercourse) the thirteenth youngest child of fifteen siblings. He lived a family-oriented life under the nourishing roof of his hard-working parents. Pace's parents attempted to invest their own good morals, values, and Christian beliefs into their children. Some of their children benefited from their wisdom, and some did not. One strong value Pace's parents emphasized was the value of an education. Education could pave a smoother road for Pace, off of the family's farmland to gainful professional employment in the city.

After being granted his Bachelor's of Science degree from their local state university, Pace was awarded a two-year full tuition and housing scholarship up north at an Ivy League University for a Master's degree. The prayers of the church parish had been answered. Pace was overwhelmed by the generosity of his kinfolk, friends, and church family who contributed the additional money and sundries necessary for him to succeed up north at college.

The fourteen-hour automobile trip was both exciting and scary. Pace felt a little like Dorothy Gale being transported from Kansas to the Land of Oz in the midst of a twister. Pace and his uncle, who drove him north, felt a swelling emptiness as the countryside quilted pattern changed from familiar open roads, farms, cattle, and harvest fields to a motif of striking brick dwellings, cement roads, traffic lights, and high-rises. Pace thought, "Toto, we're not in Kansas anymore."

Uncle returned home by bus after five days of helping Pace settle into his graduate student housing place and completed his registration and orientation to the university. His graduate studies went well, but Pace's breathing was often shadowed by isolation and fear. After a year-and-a-half, his sense of emptiness was now deepened by his feelings of loneliness, displacement, and want. He was all alone in the city, yet did not want to return to the farm after graduating.

Pace was attracted to a local Methodist church and to a fraternity on campus. Both fellowships introduced him to some life long friendships and provided him the companionship that felt like home.

One of the brothers at his church was also from his small home town and Pace was honored to serve as the best man in his homeboy's June wedding. There was a beautiful spring engagement party held off campus and Pace arrived early to assist with any heavy moving assignments that the ladies had for him. Pace drove a church deacon to the affair. As they approached the porch of the modest middle-class home address described on the invitation, one of the wedding hostesses answered the door wearing an outfit and wig only suitable for "Mr. Blackwell's B List." That was the first sign.

Pace and the Deacon entered the gala gathering and with the completion of introductions, Pace learned that the hostess's name was Esther. During the course of the evening Esther focused her time and attention on Pace. The attention felt warm, intimate and personable to him. Their conversation during the next four hours was an exchange of pleasantries and superficialities about their careers, social activities, hobbies and mutual friends in the room. Esther's speech and movement was provocative. Pace was seduced by Esther's spirituality, and the sound of his name flowing from her lips—"Pace darling." Pace was excited and sexually aroused, by her touch of his hand and the crossing of her thighs.

They exchanged telephone numbers and agreed to catch a movie and dinner on Friday after his midday examination. Pace was punctual but Esther was nearly forty-five minutes late; citing that she had to meet with her supervisor and union steward at work which caused her to miss the earlier bus. Esther teasingly stated "But I'm worth the wait," and hurried into her subsidized housing apartment to complete her afternoon meditation, clear a place for Pace to sit, and to change out of her work uniform. That was the second sign.

The telephone rang and by the one-sided conversation Pace concluded it was Esther's elderly widowed mother who apparently needed a ride to a relative's home. What remarkable timing! Esther asked, and Pace, being the gentleman that he was raised by his mother to be, reluctantly agreed. Pace thought that maybe they could still catch the 7:30 P.M. movie theatre and still transport Esther's mother. This was the third forewarning. Pace recognized none of the signs.

Due to the lateness of the evening Esther suggested they should have dinner in lieu of the movie. Esther didn't fair well with domestic chores, and kept nothing in her refrigerator but water, juice, nuts and apples. Although being sensitive to his limited graduate student stipend, Pace agreed and saw the dinner table as an opportunity to get to know Esther better. No problem, since Esther dominated the conversation and skillfully redirected any drifting reference about Pace back to herself with a touch on Pace's hand. He was a healthy male, and again, he was easily aroused. Esther enjoyed her vegetarian special as Pace dined on his baked chicken breast. These were the fourth warning signs.

The eleventh hour arrived and both nodded in agreement to leave the restaurant and venture home. The drive home was pleasant as both discussed their dreams of having good paying jobs, getting married, and maybe, having children, if God so willed. Pace would reach out to touch Esther's hand, but she modestly would withdraw her hand as if to protect her innocence. Pace walked Esther to her front door and gently kissed her left cheek. He was smitten with her smell, independence, and grace. And so, in the ensuing months before his homeboy's wedding, Pace and Esther began a courtship.

Pace was open, honest and forthcoming. Esther was superficial, illusory, and sexually provocative. They were self-contained as they enjoyed pleasurable dating, and intentionally remained out of the sight of those who knew them best. They wanted to relax from the demands of life and enjoy each other without the opinionated interference of family members and friends. These were the sixth set of warning signs.

The June garden wedding sparked several new romantic relationships, including that of Pace and Esther. Pace was looking forward to graduating before Christmas; having been offered a city job he interviewed for that month, he was feeling hopeful.

The future was bright and full of childlike dreams and hopes. In the midst of the June wedding festivities Pace told Esther that he loved her sense of spirituality, devotion to meditation and home-based lifestyle. He asked her to marry him, primarily because he lusted for her and Esther was chaste. He could not contain himself so he felt he should marry her for it was not better for him to continue to "burn." Without hesitation or reservation Esther said "Yes" and arranged to meet her girlfriends at the reception in the ladies room in order to brag about her newest "Mr. Right." Pace was "the one" she had been waiting for. This was the seventh sign.

The next six months were full with wedding plans, as Pace secured employment, and financed the majority of the wedding cost. Pace's parents met Esther by telephone and regretted that they were not able to travel to the ceremony. However, three of Pace's brothers and three of his sisters journeyed north, and drew more concerned after each encounter with Esther. They found her selfish, negative, judgmental and spoiled. The family shared their thoughts and feelings with Pace during the premarital week but Pace only proclaimed his love for her. Pace was a product of a large core family and driven by partnerships and companionships. He was twenty-six, alone, and burning.

The next ten years for Pace were an unbelievable nightmare. Within three years Esther exercised the option of resigning her employment position in lieu of being fired. It appeared that she could never verify having a college degree, license, or certification for her employment post that she held for the past prior four years. Her employer was providing her educational reimbursement fringe benefits but Esther apparently continued to register for and then drop her classes, retaining the reimbursement. Pace became the official uncompensated taxi driver for his mother-in-law and other family members. There was nearly twenty-thousand dollars of credit card debt and a threat of eviction due to the unsuitable condition of their subsidized apartment. Esther refused marital counseling, individual psychotherapy and any medication regime, citing "religious reasons." Pace grew near to Christ, and Sunday worship service, while Esther elected to rest and meditate in the quietness of their home. Esther appeared to change religious affiliations like the batteries in the home fire alarm, about two to three times each year. Esther moved into the reserved baby's room the fourth year as she grew tired of Pace's pressure for sex, intimacy and starting a family that she didn't want.

Pace was faithful, respectful, and reverent, but he felt annoyed, powerless, dehumanized and alienated in the marriage. He was hardworking, prayerful and goal-directed, but felt incompetent as a victim of Esther's constant verbal criticism. He was proud, self-empowered and assertive, but appeared inferior and intimidated by Esther. He was merciful, generous, and compassionate. But in actuality, he was neglected, forgotten and overlooked by Esther, within and outside of the marital home.

Feeling depressed, hopeless, and distraught he placed a telephone call to his fraternity brother, who created a place to which Pace could escape. As he packed, Esther seduced him with sex and made a mountain of promises, that if kept would be the answer to Pace's prayers. So he stayed and eight weeks later Esther learned that she was pregnant. Pace and Esther would never touch or sleep together again.

Pace was conflicted and convicted. He was conflicted by Esther's promises that were short lived and never materialized into permanent changed behavior. Esther continued to have a closed spirit that erected a wall of resistance and silence. She cut off verbal, physical, and sexual communication with Pace, resulting in his further frustration and distress.

Pace Jr. was born and due to his strong convictions, Pace took family leave from his job to raise and nurture his male child. The event of giving birth motivated Esther to return to the work force immediately, something Pace had not been able to persuade her to do in four years. Esther was absent any resemblance of maternal instincts. In contrast, Pace was a nourishing, loving and caring parent of strong morals, values and Christian conviction. Pace stayed with Esther for Junior but by the baby's sixth birthday, Pace grew to believe that the verbal cruelty, nonsupport, lack of respect, and lack of sex was too much to bear.

He talked with his son and explained what a divorce meant. Pace worked to impress upon his son that he was not the cause of the divorce. Pace assured Junior that he remained his loving father. Pace retained a divorce attorney, signed the divorce complaint with ex parte Orders, and ushered the process server into the house to serve Esther with the papers. Pace had secretly packed his essentials, had them stored in the trunk of his automobile, and telephoned his fraternity brother that he was on his way. With a sad heart and wet tearful face he kissed and held tight to Junior as if that boy child gave him life. Junior cried, but through his tears agreed to continue to have Pace drive him to school each morning. As he left the apartment, his breathing was shallow from fear and despair.

Utilizing the marital assets, Esther secured an attorney who filed an answer and counter complaint asking for everything, including the kitchen sink. It was on. To gain peace and sanity, Pace agreed to give Esther sole custody of Junior, asking in return for reasonable parenting time, joint legal custody, and adherence to statutory guidelines for child support. Pace accepted all of the financial obligations, and consented to Esther receiving fifty percent of the nominal marital assets. He was willing to pay the price for freedom.

Esther's behavior at the Divorce Settlement Conference was bizarre with unorthodox statements of religious preoccupation and paraphernalia. The proofs were placed on the record. The judge glanced toward Pace and granted the divorce. Pace murmured "Hallelujah—Thank you Jesus." The judge nodded and smiled. Esther's attorney departed from her, as if he was ashamed that anyone would associate him with Esther.

Pace found himself divorced, irritable, and hurt, with concentration difficulties and an inability to sleep. He found it difficult to socialize and date others. His rambled thoughts included many distressing recollections about his marriage; the vivid images haunted him. These flashbacks usually caused Pace intense distress and emotional withdrawal. Pace felt detached emotionally, and he found it difficult to talk about marriage—or to love again.

Are you on the church pew with Nia and Pace?

Nia   Pace

The Profile of Carol

Carol was a courteous, reverent and respected Southern lady. As a child she was teachable and quickly learned the value of staying focused on personal goals and appreciating the value of a simple, self-sufficient life. She accepted Jesus Christ as her Lord and Savior at the age of seven, growing steadily in God's grace and anointing. Carol possessed the gifts of administration, teaching, helps and exhortation. She lived to satisfy the Holy Scriptures.

That is the simple picture that Carol would have you believe.

The truth is that Carol had four brothers, three sisters and was the sixth oldest child of this original biological sibship. All of her siblings were deceased with the exception of her older protective brother who was in failing health. She was born in rural Tennessee and after the age of five she was raised in Birmingham, Alabama.

The 1951 core family circle was full with two adults and eight children in a modest four-bedroom rent-to-own house. There were no observed fights between Carol's mom and dad. Instead there were healthy and lively "futuristic discussions."

Carol's mom and dad were committed to discuss and resolve problems each and every day so that there would be no need to discuss those troubles or issues in the "future." Futuristic discussions kept the marital relationship honest and it kept them accountable to each other.

There was a lot of love in Carol's family home. The joy was rampant, although the seven-room house was crowded. The joy, love, respect and honor made it feel cozy. It also helped that each family member had a full life outside of the house, so rarely were all members home at the same time. The one exception was the Sunday family dinner after church. Carol's mother insisted that all of her children and her husband attend church and share Sunday dinner together. There was no need to inquire about the Sunday dinner menu. The fixings were always the same; fried chicken, mixed greens, fried corn, cornbread, candied yams, kool-aid and sweet potato pie.

After the death of her father at approximately twelve years old, Carol's mother moved the family north to highly populated, urban Detroit to seek educational and employment opportunities. There, Carol felt just as restricted as she had down south. She didn't like the fact that she and the girls had to be on the porch by sun down, while the boys were allowed to fly off to return home at their discretion. The gender bias developed in Carol a spirit of confrontation and insurrection. She longed for independence, social parity and privilege. Carol became as tough as the boys and soon she became as rebellious, self-directed, oppositional and defiant as her brothers. She made it difficult for her mother to successfully rationalize why the girls were being restricted while the boys were allowed to roam free.

Carol's thirst for freedom came at a price. At the age of seventeen and a few months before passing to the twelfth grade, she found herself pregnant. The shame was overpowering and caused Carol to make some self-destructive decisions. She was motivated to live independent of her mother's house and to personally provide for her child. Carol chose to drop out of high school, marry the man who fathered her child, and cry away her hurt and fear.

The marriage was purely based on Carol's need for financial security and her husband's need for a homebound, domestic wife. Carol's husband was insecure, abusive, and controlling. After all, Carol was a Southern lady raised to be a homebound girl. Carol's husband's marital "modus operandi" became clear within the first year. He was sexually promiscuous, alienated from Carol and their child, and rarely home. When together they would argue and he became physically abusive toward Carol. Nearly forced out by frustration, assault, and battery, within two years of marriage Carol was divorced with a child at the tender age of nineteen years old. So much for the freedom to soar like her brothers.

Carol and her baby returned to her mother's house. This time she praised the Lord for the privilege to sit on the front porch and be still. The value of being a homebound girl was fully revealed. While sitting on her porch she saw him: a handsome young man, perhaps five years her senior. Each day about half past five in the evening he would walk home from work past Carol's front porch and say "hello." He was noticed and remembered. Carol found herself looking for him at neighborhood baseball games, the movies, the corner grocery store and at church. She found him and befriended him.

He was a Southern gentleman. Carol's new beau courted her with her mother's blessings and under the watchful eye of her brothers. Carol and her beloved were more like a brother and sister than romantic partners. She and Willie married after two years of courtship and were committed to living a God-centered life. Willie became a dedicated father to Carol's oldest child and two other children that they had together.

For thirty years Carol and Willie grew in the application of the Holy Scriptures in spite of the unceasing trials and tribulations of life. Their Christian character was distinctive in the community. Their love and uncompromising dedication to each other was a beautiful sight to witness. They indeed were loving marital servants to each other.

Because of rich food, a retiring lifestyle and poor health practices, Willie was diagnosed with four life-threatening conditions, including diabetes, high blood pressure and blocked arteries of the heart. Willie had successful emergency open-heart surgery and he celebrated their twentieth wedding anniversary in his hospital bed. God was merciful and good to restore his health and deliver him back to the loving and caring arms of Carol. After a period of rehabilitation and healthy lifestyle changes, Willie resumed most of his activities, including his lawn care service. All was well. Over the following ten years, Carol's fear of losing Willie subsided and once again she could imagine them growing old and senile together.

It was a Monday evening and, as usual, Carol was running late for Bible study with her sister deaconesses at the church. Willie had finished his lawns for the day. Carol knew her husband's work routine. But this day, Willie appeared to be more meticulous than usual. The trailer that hauled the lawnmower was placed at a perfect angle, the cover over the tools completely sealed them, and the tie belts were done in a life saving knot. Willie's work was finished. The tools of the trade were secured for the next set of working hands.

Carol hastily walked to the car garage, kissed Willie good-bye, got into her automobile and dashed off to church. She rolled down her driver's window and waved at Willie as she backed out of their driveway. He always waved back and threw her a farewell kiss. This is what they always did. Everything appeared normal.

Bible study was eerie in retrospect. The pastor conducted a deep and nontraditional study of Ruth 1:6-22 with a unique focus on what spiritual characteristics were necessary for widows to daily glean the grain dropped by the wealthy. The Bible lesson reminded Carol about her last days in Alabama after the death of her father. For a while the family had to wear hand-me-down clothing from neighbors until Carol's mother secured a domestic housekeeping job for a local rich family. Although Carol appreciated the generosity of her neighbors and her mother's rich employer, she resented the teasing she suffered from her schoolmates. She vowed to never wear the clothing of others as an adult. She vowed not to glean, but instead to always be a blessing to others who are in need. Willie made that promise possible. Willie was very generous with his resources and flowered Carol with gifts far beyond her basic needs. The biblical lesson that Monday night brought past blessings to Carol's remembrance and all the way home she praised the Lord for her charitable husband.

At 9:15 P.M. she traveled home with a grateful heart. She praised the Lord with happy tears that flowed down her beautiful cheeks and settled around her chin. Carol looked forward to kissing Willie's husband face and telling him, once again today, how much she appreciated and loved him.

Willie was sitting at the back of the trailer and Carol called out to him. Carol said—"Willie, Willie." He said nothing. Carol saw him, felt his stillness, immediately telephoned 911 and the Emergency Medical Service Advance Response Unit appeared within seven minutes.

God appeared to bless her with everything that she needed to survive the moment. She was tearful as each minute swelled with fear. A strong tsunami-like wave of fear overpowered her, and a loud apparition proclaimed, "I am taking your husband and you are going to be alone." Their little dog mourned and groaned as he lay at the end of the walk way. He felt death.

Willie was transported to the emergency department of the nearby hospital. At the hospital Carol felt numb and she wondered what she was going to do next. Carol was told that despite their efforts Willie died from a heart attack in the emergency room at 10:32 P.M.

It instantly occurred to Carol that everything Willie did with his lawn tools that day—the meticulousness with which he placed every tool in its rightful spot—indicated he wasn't going to be with her anymore. She still feels numb to this day. Carol is homebound and has lost her desire to soar.

For the next few days Carol deliberately submerged herself in the funeral arrangements. Taking care of the celebration of Willie's life became her preoccupation and her comfort. The southern lady was gracious and solemn, just like her mother would expect her to be. The order of service was warm and spirited, and the gravesite honor was conclusive, final and bone-chilling.

Carol appreciated the family dinner provided at the church after the burial, but she sensed a pull on her spirit. She was compelled to return home. She was driven to return to those familiar items that she associated with Willie. Carol was moved to return to his bedroom closet that still held his smells. It was a way to get close to Willie in a way that she could not experience at the church funeral or the cemetery. To this day, she has not been able to alter anything in his closet. Carol's rationalization is that she is waiting for Willie's brother to come and select the clothing he wants. Willie's brother is elderly, disabled and lives several states away. To keep Willie's bedroom closet intact is her way of keeping Willie near.

Carol now rises each morning, says her prayers and reads the Holy Scriptures. Her precious little dog is her only companion. She gets fully dressed and sets her course for the day based on God's will. Carol's lifestyle includes only Bible study, prayer meetings, Christian fellowship, active service in three ministries of the church, and occasional visits with her family members and friends. Nonetheless, Carol feels like she is still sitting in the emergency waiting room feeling numb and she continues to ask herself "What am I going to do next?"

Are you on the same church pew with Nia, Pace, and Carol?

Nia   Pace   Carol

Chapter Two

Divorce Recovery

Fifty-one percent (51%) of those who get married get divorced in America (Barna, 2004). The five most common grounds of divorce are:

1. Adultery (Matthew 5:31)

2. Fornication (I Corinthians 7:2)

3. Desertion (I Corinthians 7:3)

4. Unequally Yoked Marital Relationships (I Corinthians 7:10-16)

5. Marital, Emotional, Physical or Psychological Abuse (Leviticus 19:17; Luke 17:3)

Malachi 2:16 declares that God hates divorce. But whether you decide to divorce or have that decision made for you, we want to remind you that you can still make choices. You can allow yourself to be destroyed by divorce, or you can choose to use this transitional phase to grow and soar. This redemptive divorce recovery period can be a time for self-examination and realign your life with God. As you successfully travel this path to recovery it is important that you:

- Recognize who you married,

- Confess your sins in the marriage,

- Forgive yourself for marrying such a person,

- Forgive them for who they were in the marriage,

- Develop persistence and a sense of purpose in life,

- Renew your mind and emotions in reference to God and not man,

17

- Minister to others who share your same hurt and pain, and

- Train yourself to image a great and awesome God who literally has his loving arms of protection around you as he holds you close in the safety of his bosom.

Remember that you were not born solely for the purpose of marriage. Rather, you were born to accomplish something in the kingdom of God. Let us examine some ways that you can set yourself free and learn how to rise from the ashes of divorce and fly to a higher level of existence.

Bitterness

After the divorce, Pace couldn't hear Esther's voice or the mention of her name without being vexed in his spirit. He felt deep seated resentment and relentless, bitter anger for wasting ten years of his life with a woman who ridiculed him and caused him to feel inadequate with her negative facial expressions, body language, lack of affection, and words that hurt. Pace was constantly nagged, criticized and lied to. He grew bitter and had thoughts of her ill-will. Pace was, understandably, bitter and angry. Bitterness is prolonged retributive anger toward another person because of an offense committed, and that described Pace. Esther offended Pace and he became bitter.

Divorce is painful and if you allow it, the anger and bitterness left in its wake can leave you feeling like there is acid in your veins. But just like you divorced your spouse, you must similarly divorce pain, because if you acquiesce to it that very pain will leave you feeling regret, cold and aloof. It will leave you glazed with hatred, hostility, grief and sarcasm. It will cause you deep distress, resentment and emotionless. It will result in your being vindictive, disagreeable, bitter and vexed in your mind and spirit.

Pace, like the rest of us, must embrace the concept that we may initially experience anger, sadness, bitterness, or a variety of other negative emotions and ungodly thoughts. But we can become mentally strong and empowered to immediately select healthier, more godly emotions and thoughts. We must conceive and believe that we have the power to choose our responses. We must grasp the notion that no one can "*make* you mad, and no one can *make* you angry." We must resolve to have a personal commitment to ourselves that although our initial reaction to an offense is weak, we will abate those emotions, gird up our loins and elect healthier and more godly feelings, thoughts and reactions in the midst of the offense. We must have a made-up mind to relate to our offenders in this manner. We must learn the lesson of Jacob. He was fearful of his reunion with his brother Esau who promised to kill him, but prayed and collected his thoughts just before the reunion, eliminating his fear of facing his adversary (Genesis 32:1-21).

Secondly, imagine, if you will, that the offender is at a distance from you on a television scene. What do we do when we don't like the television program? We turn the channel to another station—to another program. And what do we do when we can't turn the television off or pull the plug safely from the electrical circuit? We ignore the television scene until we are ready or able to leave the room or the area. Have wisdom and don't make a practice of expressing your thoughts and emotions to evil and ungodly people on the television scene and expecting them to appropriately respond back to you. Ignore them. Your premeditated mind-set should be peaceful, and you must constantly monitor and revise your feelings. Know, feel, and immerse yourself with the power source of the Holy Spirit inside you.

We must train our minds. We must replace the negative thoughts with other kinds of thoughts, or the negative thoughts will come back. "Fix your thoughts on what is true and honorable and right. Think about things that are pure and lovely and admirable. Think about the things that are excellent and worthy of praise" (Philippians 4:8 NLT).

And finally, it may be difficult at this point, but you must grow to see your former spouse or offender through the eyes of Jesus. Jesus loves them despite their lack of repentance, damaging and senseless free-will choices, unholy behavior, and immoral conduct., Yes, God still loves them. And that same God loves you. We should not destroy who God loves. We should not ruin, defame, frustrate, put down or upset those whom God loves. Our prayers and our tongues should bless those that are cursed, and bless those that curse us.

This is a good time to take a deep breath and find the inner peace within you.

To dissolve the bitterness within you remember to:

- Touch the inner core of peace within yourself. Touch your inner comfort zone, the Holy Spirit.

- Don't destroy what God loves.

- Look for godliness in your offender.

- Meditate before you speak or engage with your former spouse or friend.

- Avoid engaging with unholy offenders whenever possible.

- Give yourself time to heal and learn how to best relate to those who have caused you pain.

Forgiveness

From our humble spirit and confession flows forgiveness. Now forgiveness is not a natural action; it is contrary to our nature. We must bind and conform our mind and will. With time, our emotions will line up with our conformed thoughts. If we wait until we emotionally feel like forgiving someone, forgiveness may not ever come. Read the 37th Psalm and find strength from it and then humble yourself and commit your ways into the Lord, conform your mind, and take delight in the presence of the Lord. Entrust everything to control and guidance of the Lord. Convince yourself that God could work out all things if you were to show patience. Matthew 6:15 tells us "if ye forgive not men their trespasses, neither will your Father forgive our trespasses."

You should pray for those who have hurt you. Such dedicated prayer can lead to forgiveness by softening their heart and calming your spirit, allowing you to see that person through the eyes of Jesus. In II Corinthians 5:18, we see that Jesus has given each of us the ministry of reconciliation, which is restoring ourselves with each other and aligning ourselves with Jesus. But reconciliation is not necessarily the result of forgiveness. Reconciliation is a mutual act in which both forgive each other and restore the relationship. In other words, you can forgive your offender and still not be reconciled if the offender is in denial, hostile, or defiant and fails to repent of their own sins.

More often it is our energized anger that is the stronghold and yolk on our ability to forgive our offenders. Behind our anger are underlying feelings of:

- Hurt about offenses done against us in the past;
- Frustration about events and issues occurring in the present; and/or
- Fear about what may happen to us or our significant others in the future.

Thus we must not dwell on the anger but instead identify and process what is the base cause of our hurt, frustration and/or fear. To help you get started, answer these questions:

1. What is your first memory of feeling angry/hurt/frustration/ fear in romantic relationships?

2. What caused you to have these emotions?

3. Have these emotions sapped your energy? How?

4. Have they damaged your spirit? How?

5. Have they damaged or lessened your motivation to do what you want to do, should do, or need to do? How?

6. Have they kept you from performing at your highest level of functioning or fully exercising your God given gift(s)? How?

7. How do you prefer to be now? How do you prefer to feel? How do you prefer to act?

8. What do you *believe you need to do* now to eliminate the feelings of anger/hurt/frustration/fear from you life?

9. What can you *commit to do* now toward eliminating the anger/hurt/frustration/fear that you feel?

10. How will you achieve or implement that plan beyond today?

11. What can you do this week towards eliminating anger/hurt/ frustration/fear from your life?

To gain peace, focus, mental control, and a free spirit we must move to forgive those that have deliberately, unknowingly, or unfairly hurt us. We must proceed to face, cope with and resolve our frustration, annoyances, irritations, disappointments, and feelings of discontent.

We must change our perception on the probabilities of the future so that we can live without fear, anxiety, and apprehension. We must hold on to the biblical truth that "…God hath not given us the spirit of fear; but of power, and of love, and of a sound mind" (II. Timothy 1:7).

Your offenders may be living or deceased, but your greatest enemy is probably yourself. Forgiveness requires that you have a made-up-mind to accept yourself, your past poor judgments, and your past wrong doings. Forgiveness also requires that you have a strong personal conviction to accept your offenders for who they actually are and accept them as they present themselves to be. You should not accept or view your offenders based on what you believe may be their potential.

Forgiveness does not require the offender to acknowledge their misdeed nor does the forgiveness process require that they request forgiveness from you. When at all possible it is wise to practice the conflict resolution process designed between Christians as discussed in Matthew 18:15, in which you take successive witnesses to confront the offender if they do not acknowledge their offense. But, if one is not a believer, forgiveness does not require having dialogue with the offender who may be oppositional, defiant and resistant to your perceived truth. Be humble and open to the possibility that your perspective may not match the perspective of your offender. Truth and facts are perceived differently by people based on their personal motivation, investment, perception, personality, knowledge, skills, and experience. Bear in mind that only God knows the real facts.

Failure to forgive your offenders is dangerous to you, for it can lead to:

- Hurt
- Frustration

- Fear
- Anger
- Sadness
- Bitterness
- Aggression
- Withdrawal
- Medical, physical and emotional damage
- Legal consequences if you decide to enact revenge
- Damage to the spirit, mind and soul

Psalms 66:18 tells us "If I regard iniquity in my heart, the Lord will not hear me." We must first recognize the unholy, ungodly anger and bitterness that we personally have harbored in our heart before God will hear our prayers for healing and happiness. We know that your pain may still be great today. And if this is so, then we encourage you to move to the point that you can open your heart to the command of God to forgive your former spouse, lover or friend. This is on a higher spiritual realm. You can move your free-will to that point "if you listen to these commands of the Lord your God and carefully obey them, the Lord will make you the head and not the tail, and you will always have the upper hand" (Deuteronomy 28:13 NLT). Time will not heal your broken heart if you fail to transform your thoughts and your emotions. But peace can come by obeying God's commandments to confess your sins and forgive. Welcome peace in your life by being the head in the situation with the upper hand and not the tail.

Paul instructs us best about our sense of entitlement when he wrote "your attitude should be the same that Christ Jesus had. Though he was God, he did not demand and cling to his rights as God. He made himself nothing, he took the humble position of a slave, and appeared in human form" (Philippians 2:5-7 NLT). Just let it go.

To forgive our offenders we must lay aside our sense of entitlement to revenge and choose to view the wrongdoer through the eyes of mercy, grace, and agape love. Like Jesus, we must be forgiving, merciful, just, and separate from sin. Forgiveness does not mean that we will thoroughly forget the offense. But it does mean that we lose all signs and symptoms of preoccupation, anger, bitterness, hurt, frustration, and fear associated with our offender and their offensive acts.

Don't confuse forgiveness with trust. Trust must be earned. Forgiveness may not be enough to get us back on track; we may have to realign our relationship with the offender so that we can best protect ourselves from their selfish acts. And to better protect our hearts, it is important that we not invest more in a person than we are willing to lose.

Forgiveness will yield honesty, integrity, and acceptance of reality. Forgiveness revises our faith and hope. Forgiveness enables us to surrender our personal will to God, and come to trust God as our sole source of strength and protection. Forgiveness rewards us with peace, joy, and an open spirit. The wisdom of humility and forgiveness will produce an inner freedom and release from the control that our former spouses, friends, lovers, offenders, and enemies hold on our sense of happiness and satisfaction.

Confession and Humility

It is important to know the relationship between confession, pride and humility in our efforts to repent of our wrongdoings, and recognize the emotional baggage we carry in and out of romantic relationships. We're not talking about the pride described as a "haughty spirit" that "goes before a fall" (Proverbs 16:18), but instead the pride that reflects self respect. This kind of pride is essential in romantic relationships that are building a spirit of collaboration in order to sustain love and affection in the relationship. Pride ensures satisfaction and personal fulfillment. It promotes longevity and survival of romantic relationships. Partners who have pride in a romantic relationship will experience less conflict and confusion in. Partners who have personal pride are more protective of their jointly felt needs, desires, and goals.

Then there is pride's dark side, the side we mentioned earlier. Taken to its human extreme, pride can hinder our willingness and ability to confess our wrongdoings.

So where is the balance? To keep pride from going into excess, we must actively practice confession and humility. Confession and humility reduce tension and arguments. Outsiders may view it as weakness, but confession and humility are a strength in romantic relationships. It's good to be humble; you just may be wrong!

The operative word here is balance, balance, balance. If both partners do not practice mutual submission, abuse and neglect are the all-to-common consequences. Partners with an excess of pride can become physically, verbally and emotionally abusive when their partner refuses to meet their own personal needs *as requested*. Even if pride is not the problem, partners may simply neglect meeting each others' needs because neither of them is cognizant of the importance of considering the other first. In the process, basic needs in the romantic relationship go unmet, resulting in bitterness and unresolved differences which carry into future relationships if they are not resolved. Bitterness from unresolved issues is the emotional baggage that we tag and carry.

True Repentance

"I'm so sorry I cheated on Linda," Thomas offered to their marriage therapist. "Things just haven't been the same; my life is a mess now, and I just wish I could get it back."

Linda wasn't happy with Thomas's statement of 'repentance.' Why? Because it wasn't real repentance! Far too often we express remorse, regret and repent only about the consequences of our free-will choices. And too often, if there are no negative consequences or confrontations by others, then there is no felt guilt, and subsequently, no repentance.

We must learn to separate the assessment of our initial behaviors from the assessment of our final consequences. We must repent our initial sinful behaviors, whether or not the consequences are concealed or exposed, whether the consequences are known or unknown, or whether the consequences are good or bad.

Repentance means to confess our sins which is examining the source of the sin or offense and not just apologizing for the aftermath. For James 5:16 tells us to confess our faults one to another, and pray one for another that we may be healed. To cleanse our soul and spirit, we must confess and repent our sins and unholy behaviors regardless of the consequences. We must be committed to do what is godly and immediately repent the unholy source of our motivation—repent the ungodly heart that initiates our behavior and actions. Repentance by our free-will choice is more redemptive than our mere verbal apology about consequences for our voluntary acts. To be free from toxic relationships and interpersonal relationship pain, we need to be free from what has distressed or harmed us. We need to be free of irreligious thought, emotions, behaviors and actions. We need to be redeemed through the repentance of our sins.

Healing

Jacob was left all alone in the camp, and a man came and wrestled with him until dawn. When the man saw that he couldn't win the match, he struck Jacob's hip and knocked it out of joint at the socket. Then the man said, "Let me go, for it is dawn." But Jacob panted, "I will not let you go unless you bless me." What is your name?" the man asked. He replied "Jacob." Your name will no longer be Jacob," the man told him. "It is now Israel, because you have struggled with God and men and have won." "What is your name?" Jacob asked him. "Why do you ask?" the man replied. Then he blessed Jacob there. (Genesis 32:24-29 NLT)

Jacob was like many of us who are in a spiritual struggle and in need of a healing from our wounds. Our spiritual struggles and emotional pain have mounted over time, as a result of our inexperienced relationship to God and poor relations with others. Our struggles leave us with emotional baggage and mental scars. When we heal and strengthen our relationship with God, we will gain the wisdom necessary to heal our relationships with others. Our struggles and scars are a reminder of our past hurts, pains and injustices. They are a reminder of our own sinful thoughts and behaviors. Often when we feel that we can't win in struggles, we fight back and hurt others. And such fights with our former spouses, lovers and friends will leave us feeling out-of-joint and out-of-balance, like Jacob. But even that feeling is a blessing, because it simply reveals our need for God. "Trust in the Lord with all thine heart; and lean not unto thine own under-standing. In all thy ways acknowledge him, and he shall direct thy path" (Proverbs 3:5-6).

God can not bless you in the midst of your personal unholy wars, battles and struggles with former spouses, lovers and friends. God can not bless you on top of your persistent sinful mess. Let it go and move on to the next phase of your God-directed life. With humility, confession, and forgiveness, make the transition from a place of pain and struggle to a healing place in Him.

A transitional phase may feel like a period of confinement or in-carceration; or you can view it as an anointed period of restoration in which you can bring your spirit to God. In your period of transition, you can restore your vertical fellowship with God and your horizon-tal fellowship with others—yes, even former spouses, lovers, friends and offenders.

We're told that as Jacob left Peniel the sun rose and he was limping because of his injured hip (Genesis 32:30-31). We are prayer-ful that you can see the blessings that result from your struggles and scars. You have God's favor and grace that arises from your out-of-joint limbs and emotional pain. The sun will rise on you, blessing you with God's hope and deliverance. Let the rising of the sun remind you that the comfort of the Holy Spirit can also rise inside of your heart. Let the rising of the sun prompt your memory that Jesus "was wounded and abused for our sins. He was beaten so that we might have peace. He was whipped and we were healed" (Isaiah 53:5). You do not need to struggle with others and die in your spirit. Jesus has already struggled and died for you on the cross. Atone your sins and be healed. The nails that held Jesus up on the cross will also hold you.

PERSONAL TESTIMONY:

It has been a blessing to be raised by Aunt Bernice Finner-McAdoo and Aunt Thelma Jean White-Finner who are exceptional educated and licensed registered nurses. Recently while recovering from major abdominal surgery I found myself nearly bedridden and in a state of awesome pain and discomfort. The surgery went well as planned, but the wounds were difficult to view. My husband Robert was a warrior; changing the surgical gauzes that was stressful for me as I looked at hanging drainage tubes, tender skin, and discoloration of my body that was unimaginable, but evidently true.

It appeared so unproductive to stop my professional life, lie still on my back, and be resigned to merely completing a daily wound management and medication regime for six weeks. The wounds made me look ugly and unattractive. I was convinced there was something wrong with me and that I would never get better or heal properly. I was reminded of my trauma two to three times a day as I changed the surgical gauze, prompting numerous panic telephone calls to Aunt Bernice and Aunt Thelma. I would plead for them to rush to my bedside to examine me and assess the status of my wounds once again. Because they loved me, they would abandon their responsibilities for the day and attend to my emotional pleas. They knew me like their child, and I trusted their words. Upon examination of me, and to my surprise, both of their analyses were exactly the same. They would look directly into my tear-filled eyes and proclaim "Baby—keep following the daily regime. Your outside wounds look unattractive now, but everything is going according to the doctor's plan. Remember that we heal from the inside out."

Herein lies the lesson. The devil has to confront you with your *past* sins and wounds, because he has no control over your *future*. You are a child of God and God knows you. God has a plan for your life and if you are seeking first the Kingdom of God and his righteousness, and following the Holy Spirit you are indeed getting better. You are healing and becoming a better, more holy and godlier single Christian. Just keep following God's plan for your life. Keep following his daily regime for your healing by reading God's word, praying, confessing your sins, eliminating unholiness, and joyfully living out your God-given purpose. You may not be totally pleased with all of your behaviors and personal choices now, but keep the faith. In due season you will show the outside world the behavioral improvements and righteousness for which your heart yearns. In due season, you will heal from the inside out!

"SES": Declaring Self-Empowerment and Gaining Personal Courage

A Self-Empowered Single (SES) assumes responsibility for their personal decisions by learning how to choose freely from healthy alternatives after considering the consequences of their choices. An SES takes charge of their own God-ordered destiny, happiness and lifestyle. An SES is opposed to allocating their personal power and authority to others. An SES doesn't allow their romantic partners and friends to cause them to suffer or to make unwarranted personal sacrifices. In our book, *Marital Secrets: Dating, Lies, Communication and Sex* we wrote: "There is a difference between suffering and personal sacrifice. The former is to be avoided; the latter, wisely and freely chosen. Suffering is unavoidable distress or pain, being forced to endure and sustain a personal loss or damage of something tangible or intangible. The time frame: no end in sight." And the loss just may be the soul and spirit of the SES.

However, making a personal sacrifice is surrendering something for the sake of something or someone else. A personal sacrifice is something that one gives up—a free-will choice for a greater purpose or cause. And the sacrifice is only for a given time period.

Givers frequently have a hard time telling the difference between suffering and self-sacrifice. Often, the very qualities Sole-Soul Takers are looking for in a spouse are qualities that are missing in themselves. We should be careful about what we expect in a relationship. We should not expect more in a spouse (or romantic partner) then we ourselves can provide.

SES, don't assume a dependent, babyish and childlike posture in romantic relationships. Instead, regularly articulate your personal needs and personal wants with the expectation that they will be satisfactorily met by your significant other. As an SES you must view yourself as worthy of honor, love and respect by your romantic partner.

If you are an SES, you are empowered by the power of the Holy Spirit to have:

* Wisdom, revelation, knowledge and foresight about where God is moving your life.

- A sense of engagement, mission, and tenacity in your God-given talents, gifts and abilities.

- Personal duty, responsibility and personal promise to live a happy, peaceful, purposeful, holy and godly single lifestyle.

- Reciprocity of giving and receiving between yourself and your romantic partners and friends with the intent of enhancing the quality of life for all.

- A sense of love and gratitude for God, self and tangible personal accomplishments.

As an SES, assure that you extend your hand upward to God who is your power source. As an SES resist submissive, clinging, dependent and fearful behavior. These behaviors are traps and foster dependence on romantic partners which will make it difficult to separate yourself from unhealthy, evil and ungodly people in your life.

WISDOM BOX #1:

1. Pray first and collect your thoughts.

2. Don't expect evil people to respond to you in a rational way.

3. Abort and shift ungodly thoughts to positive and constructive ideas.

4. See your offender through the eyes of Jesus.

5. Accept your offenders for who they actually are instead of judging them.

6. Understand that forgiveness is an intellectual decision and not an emotional one.

7. Don't invest more in a person than you are willing to lose.

8. Confess all sins regardless of the consequences.

9. Realize that we heal from the inside out.

Chapter Three

New Wineskins for Widows and Widowers

Wineskins were usually made of goatskin with the smooth belly skin found inside and the course tough hairy skin side held on the outside. The inside skin is sensitive to the substance it holds and the outside skin is tough and steady. The inside skin is settled and the outside skin presents a protective barrier for the gift held inside.

The wineskin is shaped and formed into a bag that can bear water, milk, or old fermented wine. Only old settled wine should be stored in old wineskins.

For new wine to ferment, the wine must move and become stirred up. It must become intense and agitated. The new wine cannot stay stagnant, docile and still if it is to become ready for consumption. New wine is subject to fermentation, a powerful pressure process. But when this new, powerful and active wine is placed in old settled wineskins, the pressure in the container will cause the old wineskins to burst at the seams. As Jesus so vividly tells us, new wine cannot be constrained into old wineskins (Matthew 9:17 NLT).

Carol's life was settled like old wine. She handled the death of her husband in a dutiful, unassertive, and amenable manner. Her way of honoring the memory of her husband was to maintain the status quo. Carol's life was dull, ho-hum, and humdrum. Her spirit had faded away with the dying breath of her husband. Her spirit was like old wineskins.

In the wisdom of ancient Egypt, mourners traditionally buried some of their tears in old wineskins with the deceased. Every widow and widower's situation is different; but Carol, and many other widows and widowers, should come to the realization that they need to bury their tears in the old wineskins of their past life. They should seek new wine, a new lifestyle, a new perspective, and a new spirit. They should give themselves permission to stir up their God given gifts and their inner spirit. They should not bridle and constrain their new opportunities in life and their chance to be happy. They should not try to transplant their new life in their old lifestyles. To do so may cause damage to their family, occupations, and homes. To live on and to enjoy a fresh start is the message of Jesus. We must leave the cemetery willing to follow Christ and be prepared for new ways of looking at things, new routines and new people in our lives. This does not dishonor the memory of our deceased spouse, but recognizes that they and we are in different, but still good, places. The latter days with God can be better than the past. The new life like new wine can be better than the familiar. Remember that at the end of the wedding in Cana, Jesus turned plain water into the best new wine with a simple dip of the cup by a servant's hand (John 2:1-12). Just like that, Jesus can turn your lifeless spirit and old memories into a happy new beginning.

What do you need in order to ferment again? What do you need to make new in your world in order to be happy, feel alive and make peace with your loss? Is it a new neighborhood or a new home? A new bed, or new painted walls? A new job, a new dress style or new hair style? Give yourself permission to identify your new needs and establish daily activities, and short term and long term goals, that will achieve your new needs. Taste how sweet life can really be.

Period of Mourning

Customs have not been served widows and widowers well. Traditionally in America, male widowers were expected to mourn only a few days to a maximum of five to six months and remarry within two years, while female widows were expected to mourn at least six to twelve months and remarry after two to three years. The other discrimination matrix is on the age difference. Younger people were expected to mourn at the minimum end of the range while older women were expected to mourn in relationship to the advancement of their age. And then there were the cultural and ethnic traditions of wearing mourning black and widow caps.

Each widow and widower's circumstances are unique and the period of mourning should be designed accordingly. The appropriate mourning period will be determined by factors such as the quality of the relationship, last interaction, length of the relationship, significance of the relationship and other individual concerns. But don't let a season of mourning turn into a lifetime of mourning. Don't view yourself as a victim of your spouse's death or as a prisoner of your past. Women are the womb for the world and men are the rod that we lean on, so know that life must go on. By the sixth month try to lighten your clothing colors, eliminate the grieving headgear, place your hand on your chest, and feel the beat of your own heart. Visualize the extending awesome hand of God literally pulling you from the chamber of spiritual despair and despondency into a beautiful present world of new beginnings and memories. Shift your thinking from your losses to the new opportunities that are toward your God-driven destiny. It is important that you don't let your painful experience become your catered pity party, floating slavery ship or new hysterical persona. Exchange your new beauty for the ashes that have remained after the ruin of your dreams. See your new beginning, claim it, feel it and live it. Life must continue to flow through you.

Living Beyond the Memories

As widows and widowers, it is very important to cherish precious memories and abandon bad memories of past relationships. In order to maintain a healthy attitude about the loss of a mate by death, it is necessary to recall events and experiences that were not only exciting but everlasting in memory. Recalling memories of excitement brings joy and happiness to the life of widows and widowers instantly. Widows and widowers are encouraged to participate in activities with others easily when memories are pleasant regarding previous mates. Talking about deceased mates is not only revealing, but it can be enjoyable. Widows and widowers often choose to collect and display items that were favorites of their deceased mates. Choosing to remember good memories and experiences is necessary to survive the painful experience of loss by death of mates. Deciding to embrace the memory of humorous experiences relieves unwanted stress, grief, anxiety, and other unanticipated feelings that suddenly occur. Try to only recall those experiences that will cause your inner spirit and face to smile until your new life is fortified.

Loneliness

Most widows and widowers will tell you that their mate's absence is the thing that looms largest. That loneliness can be abated. Spending time with friends, family, and others relieves widows and widowers of much grief and sadness. It is important to avoid the temptation to insulate or seclude yourself from others during periods of loneliness. Instead, engage in phone conversations, personal visits, and social events to avoid loneliness and feelings of despair. Also, participate in physical activities to relieve stress and anxiety and promote good physical conditioning.

Self-love is important during periods of loneliness. Do special things for yourself when you're lonely! Being good to yourself may be as simple as spa pampering with body massages, a manicure, or a pedicure. Social engagements that allow you to meet others are important to eliminate boredom and loneliness. This may include dancing, parties, church activities and visiting events in various communities. Engagement in daily prayer, as often as possible, will relieve feelings of loneliness and cause a spiritual awakening. Meditations and simple quiet time do wonders for relieving feelings of loneliness. If loneliness renders you incapable of performing routine adult activities, you may need to consult professionals with special skills such as ministers, counselors, psychiatrists, medical doctors, or psychologists.

Above all, seek God for guidance and comfort. Matthew 6:33 inform us to "seek ye first the kingdom of God, and his righteousness; and all these things shall be added unto you." Matthew 7:7 compels us to "ask and it shall be given you; seek, and ye shall find;

knock, and it shall be opened unto you." To eliminate loneliness seek God first and all your needs and desires will be fulfilled, in spite of your loss.

Companionship

"And the Lord god said, it is not good that the man should be alone; I will make him an helpmate for him...and the Lord God caused a deep sleep to fall upon Adam, and he slept; and He took one of his ribs, and closed up the flesh instead thereof; and the rib, which the Lord God had taken from man, made he a woman, and brought her unto the man" (Genesis 2:18-22).

Companionship is essential to life. When you have lost a mate due to death or divorce, you may need to somehow replace the companionship loss that is so acute right after the event. Your emotional, psychological and spiritual survival are at stake.

So...converse! Interact! Consider who is special in your circle who demonstrates self-understanding, someone who is in touch with their own pain, thoughts, feelings and needs. Look to family members and/or friends for comfort. Gravitate towards those who offer true love and affection without your having to ask for it. Gravitate towards those who are present in body, mind, and spirit for you, towards those with whom you are on one accord, towards those for whom God is their source of strength.

The responsibility of companionship rests with you. Tell others in your support system what you need, and revise that declaration as often as you need to until your day of healing comes.

Dating

After you have lost someone significant, you may want to begin dating. That's OK, and natural. But you must be cautious, especially if you begin before you are fully healed from your loss. Don't start dating before you are emotionally, spiritually, physically, and psychologically ready to engage in a new romantic relationship. That giving and receiving from a new partner takes effort, energy, and time that you will simply not have if you are not healed.

Secondly, you must clearly define your purpose and goals for dating to avoid confusion and conflict—and not be shy about communicating that to the person you are dating. How much time and energy are you willing to commit? It is important that you both are on the same page. One may want permanence, and another mere temporary companionship or friendship. To avoid further loss on top of loss, communicate with whomever you are dating!

Thirdly, you must decide the amount of risk that you will be willing to assume during the dating phase. Needless to say, no dating relationship will be without problems. Assume and expect to experience the array of positive and negative feelings that come with any relationship, from joy and delight to anger, resentment, mistrust, and bewilderment. And work not to bring your past hurts into your new relationship. Dating carries no guarantees; you must learn how to date effectively. Don't worry; this is one of those things that improve with time, if you give it your prayerful, thoughtful attention!

Wisdom Box #2

1. Stir up the new wine that God has given you.

2. Don't let a season of mourning become a lifetime of mourning.

3. Seek companionship.

Chapter Four

Before You Marry:
Breaking Strongholds, Yokes and Generational Curses

Before you even think about getting married, examine yourself. The best way to do this is in the context of your family history. The family unit is like a glazed doughnut. The glaze of the doughnut or home environment may be sweet chocolate, caramel or vanilla; or it may be tart lemon. As we pass back and forth through the powerful and nurturing hole of this imaginary "glazed doughnut," its sweet or tart taste lodges in our mouths, covering our souls and forming our spirits. The shaping of our social learning begins at birth, as we observe the behaviors of others and then attempt them, rehearse them, have them reinforced or punished, and finally repeat or eliminate them in our later lives. Behaviors and habits often are chosen according to whom we choose to model.

We all seem to find refuge and security with what is familiar and similar. We then become comfortable and fortified in these places of security. Over time, we form defeating strongholds that we lean on as our reference point of survival. Without a healthy relationship with God or without an effective clinical intervention, those detrimental *strongholds* are nourished and become unhealthy *yokes* on our lives. And then our negative strongholds and fatalistic yokes become harmful, injurious *generational curses*.

If we continue to think, feel and behave in the same manner and expect a different result then we are neither smart nor wise. The strongholds, yokes and generational curses that keep us from being happy must be broken.

The impact of our personal family histories will strongly impact the quality of our relationships, the effectiveness of our interpersonal communications and our ability to fully disclose our true selves. How we were "glazed" will determine if we will be honest, truthful, sincere and faithfully committed. The way we were "glazed" affects the quality of our thoughts, the stability of our emotions and the normality of our feelings. The way we were "glazed" will affect our level of trust, independence and ability to change. It will determine if we operate according to a work ethic. It will determine how we experience of shame, guilt, or doubt. The way we were "glazed" will influence whether we will feel inferior or have a strong ego. It will determine whether we will be able to demonstrate appropriate intimacy, whether we will hope or despair, whether we will be part of the community or sit in isolation.

If we are "glazed" sweetly, we will have hope, steadfastness, will-power, purpose, mission, and competency. If we are "glazed" sweetly we will demonstrate fidelity, faithfulness, a willingness to give and receive love, a caring spirit, wisdom and peace. On the other hand, if we were "glazed" bitterly, we may demonstrate fear, self-doubt, insecurity, inadequacies, incompetencies, uncertainties, indecisiveness and promiscuity. If we were "glazed" bitterly, we may have selfishness, dissatisfaction, meaningless living and lack a strong moral core. It is wise to thoroughly and exhaustively know the ingredients, recipe and "glazing" of your intended's "family doughnut." It is also wise to consider who has had the strongest influence on your significant other's life; for that will be the indicator of what harm or blessing will be on your relationship.

Your ability to cope with and accept the issues in your relationship and marriage will be determined by how well you understand your intended partner's personal and family history "glazing." Haven't you ever noticed that people who come from families with histories of long, quality marriages tend to form lasting, lifetime relationships?

If you don't know what a good marriage looks like, it is difficult to emulate a good marriage. You can't do what you haven't been taught. We are what we have touched, witnessed and learned.

But be encouraged; all is not lost! Deuteronomy 24:16 assures us that "The fathers shall not be put to death for the children, neither shall the children be put to death for the fathers: every man shall be put to death for his own sin." Generational curses, yokes, and strongholds can be broken. We must have what Romans 12:2 describes as a "made-up mind" not to conform to this world but to instead be "transformed by the renewing of your mind, that ye may prove what is that good, and acceptable, and perfect will of God." Your mistakes are redeemable; that is the good news of Jesus Christ!

Blame-Shifting

It is often said that we can choose our behavior, but we can not choose the consequences of those behaviors. The failure on most singles' parts is not controlling their flesh long enough to foresee, anticipate, and consider both the immediate and long term consequences of any single behavior. In the midst of immediate self gratification and sin, we show too often a reckless disregard for the natural consequences of our momentary acts. And for every action there is always a reaction.

Suddenly, we are forced to face the uncontrolled consequences that flow from our choices. Just as abruptly, we often feel unfairly judged by those who become aware of, or who are negatively affected by, our behaviors and choices. Now feeling unjustly accused we may then blame others for the consequences of our very own decisions. Poor foresight usually leads to good hindsight. But it is best to fast forward our thoughts to the future before we make our choices in the present.

Nia, like many other saved single Christians, satisfied her thirst in the moment. She gratified her need for inner peace, comfort and fulfillment with food. She failed to anticipate the long term consequences of onset of obesity, three life-threatening conditions, and a seven-year death sentence by her fiftieth birthday. When food failed to satisfy, Nia appeased her need for physical touch, attachment and ecstasy with sex with married and single men. Even so, she didn't foresee the long term consequences of massive fibroid tumors, hysterectomy and childlessness. Nia expressed her emotional discomfort with repeated traumatic romantic drama, hurt, frustration and now the fear of being alone for a lifetime. She grew to express herself with a sharp tongue, colorful cursing and persecutory nature. Despite the Word of God she heard each week, she didn't see that the long term consequences of her unhealthy emotional reactions and ungodly conduct were bitterness, unforgiveness, insecurity, and spiritual emptiness. Because of her lofty self-image, weak ego and pride, Nia could not face and accept responsibility for the natural and feasible consequences of her choices.

Twenty years later, Nia still can not see the direct relationship between her unholy choices and the damaging long term consequences of her choices. Her guilt, shame, and spiritual immaturity have hindered her ability in mid-life to accept the consequences of her young adult choices.

Sin and strongholds nourish our lack of responsibility for our deliberate acts and conduct. We love ourselves and it is very difficult to face ourselves each day with the power of guilt and shame on our back. In what areas do you experience guilt, shame and spiritual immaturity as a result of your failure to accept responsibility for the unforeseen and foreseeable consequences of your deliberate acts? To whom have you shifted the blame and held responsible for where you presently are in life?

Blame-shifting is assigning responsibility for our circumstances and outcomes to others in lieu of accepting the blame ourselves. But God holds us individually responsible for our every move, choice, behavior, thought, emotion and deed. He holds us accountable for our behaviors, just as he expects us to hold Him accountable to his covenant. We can not escape our consequences and God can not escape his promises.

Thus we must not "blame-shift" our unhappiness to our romantic partners. We must assume responsibility for who we allow ourselves to date, make love to, have children with and marry. We can not shift the blame for our unhappiness and discontent to our romantic partner's parentage or to their behavior. We must assume responsibility for each situation we allow ourselves to experience. If the relationship brings you guilt then assume responsibility. Blame yourself and end the acquaintance.

"So then, each of us will give an account of himself to God. Therefore let us stop passing judgment on one another. Instead, make up your mind not to put any stumbling block or obstacle in your brother's way" (Romans 14:12-13).

Singles, strive to become self-empowered by making responsible romantic decisions, after considering the immediate and long term consequences of your choices. Don't shift the blame to others. "Sit in humility and rise-up in responsibility" (African Proverb).

The "But" Stronghold

Get your **"but"** out of the way—**"but"** this, **"but"** that, **"but"** you don't understand, **"but"** you didn't"…And what statements do you use—"I agree with you, **but"**…"I see your point, **but"**…"I'll try that, **but"**…"I promise I will do that, **but"**…"I'll compromise with you, **but"**…

William R. Miller states that "the word **"but"** functions like an eraser, negating the motivation that went before…by understanding and paying close attention to our speech patterns, we can move ourselves from mere desire for change into commitment and action."

The "But Stronghold" is a product of wavering, indecisiveness and fear. The "But Stronghold" is one of the greatest barriers to personal change, interpersonal romantic enhancement and marital engagement. Consistent with Miller's writings, we must:

- have a desire, commitment, and motivation to change our behavior, thinking, emotions and choices.

- believe that we are capable and able to make the desired change or commitment.

- have specific reasons and arguments for or the benefits of change.

- have a personal need for the change or commitment.

Fears of Commitment

People have differing individual needs. Therefore, their level of commitment to one another varies. Often males, and, to a lesser degree, females, cannot verbalize but will exhibit why it is difficult for them to make a commitment to marry and to remain married.

In most cases, the reason is fear. Some fears are healthy and well-founded; however, irrational fears or fears based on misconceptions can hinder a person's ability to form lasting relationships. In our counseling work we have uncovered a number of fears and misconceptions about commitment. For each of these fears we provide words of guidance and suggested remedies to shatter each stronghold.

☞ **Misconceptions about the institution of marriage**.

Men and women have created the myth that the institution of marriage will be the cleansing power for all deficiencies and problems that they were subjected to in their single life. They make the mistake of believing that each day of marriage will be a good day and just loving each other will make everything right.

👍 **Remedy:** God gave marriage as a gift which serves three purposes: (1) to leave your parents and unite together in a public ceremony; (2) to accept mutual responsibility for each other's welfare and to love the mate above all others; and (3) to unite into oneness in the intimacy and commitment of sexual union that is reserved for marriage (from the *Life Application Study Bible*, New Living Translation). Strong marriages include all three elements of unity. Marriage is a calling and not merely a desire of the heart.

☞ **Fearing the loss of control over lifestyle, activities, money, body, freedom of movement, property, etc.**

✍ **Remedy:** This fear usually arises when an individual fails to focus on the fact that all that we have belongs to God, and we are merely the stewards of our earthly possessions. The remedy is to stop loving the world and all that it offers, for when we love the world, we show that we do not have the love of God— a spirit greater than ourselves. The world offers only physical pleasure and pride of possession. We should not lose focus on our status as stewards. Our material accomplishments are *not* the sole end-product of our creative hands.

☞ **Fear that marriage will become boring and that they will miss out on something in life.**

✍ **Remedy:** To maintain a healthy and rewarding relationship, an individual must learn how to be tolerant of the mediocre or boring times in a relationship or marriage and to aggressively plan to transform insecure and unexciting times into joy and happiness. You must avoid your old "haunts," especially during boring times. Turn away and go somewhere else, for evil people cannot sleep until they have done their evil deed for the day. They cannot rest unless they have caused someone like you to stumble.

☞ **Fear of feeling trapped and losing a sense of self.**

✍ **Remedy:** When you focus on developing your relationship with God, you will gain a strong sense of self and the will that God has for your life. Seek people who have that focus; it will make for an equal "yoke" and enhance your individuality.

☞ **Becoming overly critical and "picky" when deciding on a mate.**

👍 **Remedy:** As a single person, pray for an answer and always know what God has confirmed as your "bottom line," your standard for a spouse. You know the person must love the Lord and your family. You know they must be born again. You know that finances are important. You know that there is a certain way you should be treated. Then, simply trust in the Lord with all of your heart and do not be impressed with your own wisdom (see Proverbs 3:5).

☞ **Intolerance of others.**

👍 **Remedy:** You may be so stressed in your personal or professional life that you cannot bear to even be around others. Be careful here; the tendency toward this trait increases with age. To overcome intolerance, you must experience a spiritual renewal of your thoughts and attitudes. Concentrate on being kind to each other, tenderhearted, compassionate, forgiving one another, just as God through Christ has forgiven us, as described in Colossians 3:12-14. Also, it can be helpful to do a "reality check." How many people have to tolerate our own faults when they would much rather not? It's a hard question, but the answer may help you to be less persnickety.

☞ **Feeling overprotective of personal finances.**

👍 **Remedy:** The Word of God (Matthew 25:14-30) tells us that those who use well what they are given will be given even more, and they will have an abundance. It goes on to say that from those who are unfaithful, even what little they have will be taken away. The key to keep in mind is that personal finances should be disbursed responsibly, whether married or not.

☞ **Feeling too stressed-out to juggle one more thing.**

☝ **Remedy:** You will experience difficulty in handling the many balls you juggle in life each day without a sense of purpose, mission and peace. Peace of mind comes when we learn how not to worry about anything; but instead to pray about everything. Tell God what you need, and thank Him for all he has done (see Philippians 4:6-7). This requires consistent practice. And no, it is not easy.

☞ **Worrying that marriage will coerce personal change.**

☝ **Remedy:** You can't hurry love or build up to marriage too quickly. Love and marriage both require time. The proper perception is that marriage brings as a gift rewarding and positive change that allows partners to find favor with each other, as well as encourage, help, assist, uphold and foster each other.

When two people come into a relationship, there is a tendency to want to make improvements or changes in each other. Early on in the relationship a decision needs to be made—preferably by both partners—that neither can change the other into what they want each other to be. It is best to move in the direction of compromise and mutual acceptance. As the husband and wife submit to one another, they will become one spirit, one flame, and reflect each other as two lights that join together.

☞ **Clashing values and lifestyles.**

☝ **Remedy:** Adequate fellowship and dating time spent together will reveal if value and lifestyle differences are too significant to consider marriage as a feasible option. And remember, you should never want to be with anyone who doesn't want to be with you.

☞ **Feeling uncertain as to who is really going to be in control in the marriage.**

👍 **Remedy:** Those who seek a biblically-based marriage will rest assured in the Word of God that the husband is the head of his wife as Christ is the head of his Body, the Church. The husband must love his wife as he loves himself, and the wife must respect her husband and submit to her husband (see Ephesians 5:22-27). As the wife follows her husband, the husband shall follow Christ—He is the one who should really be in control of the marriage.

☞ **Lacking personal and professional success at this point in life.**

👍 **Remedy:** Remain mindful that all of us should grow to know the voice of God and meditate on His Word. The same God who takes care of us will supply all our needs from his glorious riches which have been given to us in Christ Jesus (Philippians 4:19). We should know what we want in life and what we need in order to achieve our personal and professional goals. Then, we should study, prepare and ask God for it.

☞ **Being afraid that the partner will not completely accept and support their personal goals and dreams.**

👍 **Remedy:** In marital counseling couples repeatedly remind us that they see themselves as competitors and not as partners. Instead of focusing on the acceptance of others, we should be loyal to Christ, honor Him and seek only His acceptance. We should then hold close to our breasts those that encourage, assist, and foster us in reaching our goals.

☞ **Recognizing the difficulty in finding a person who has a solid relationship with God.**

☜ **Remedy:** God's commandment to us is that we love one another as He has loved us (John 13:34). We need to understand that marriage is not just two bodies coming together, but the coming together of two spirits, two souls, and yes, two families. Love and marry your spirit complement—your soul mate. For the Christian, this is only possible with one who has a relationship with God through Jesus Christ. If your fear has to do with the fact that none of the people you encounter meet this basic requirement, your fear is healthy and well-founded.

☞ **Being unable to read people correctly and biblically.**

☜ **Remedy:** People often marry on the basis of "phileo" love that reacts to what is being done to them instead of "agape" love which is focused on the needs of the beloved. Study well who is meeting your spiritual, mental, emotional, intellectual, physical and material needs as a way to discriminate "phileo" lovers from "agape" lovers.

☞ **Fearing that a spouse will not be focused at home.**

☜ **Remedy:** Some people are unable to view the marital home as a place of refuge. Instead they see the home as a place to have physical needs met (e.g., food, shelter and sex) and personal property stored (e.g., clothing and other possessions). Such persons view their home as a "last resort" for recreation instead of the first and preferred point for their leisure activities. Study well who hastens to your side in comparison to who is with you only when it is convenient. This will tell you who views you as "home."

☞ **Lacking model marriages to emulate.**

👍 **Remedy:** Welcome an opportunity to change generational curses. An inability to form lasting marital partnerships is certainly one of the most devastating generational curses. It is essential for people who have not witnessed good marriages to find happy, spiritually focused couples and spend time with them.

☞ **Fearing a lack of honest disclosure by others, leading to a lack of trust.**

👍 **Remedy:** Study, understand and discuss with the person how others have broken the veil of trust with you since birth. Make sure they love you enough to help you heal from those wounds. If you find yourself incapable of that, seek counseling. And be careful to keep your word so that others can trust you the way you want to trust them.

☞ **Having subconscious, fear-provoking dreams about marriage.**

👍 **Remedy:** Humble yourself and freely submit to God, and you will break this stronghold of fear.

If you do not overcome your "but strongholds" and fears to commitment, then you willingly and intentionally assume the risk that those unknown areas may present a problem in your marriage. The best time to learn about the person in-depth and confront your own fears and strongholds is *before* you get married. Take the blinders off your eyes; get beyond the good feelings that you have about the person. If you feel this person is your soul mate, then do not be afraid to ask them hard questions. **If you marry prematurely, you will have to choose to accept what you did not try to learn about beforehand.**

We have developed something we call the Finner-Williams Pre-Marital Screening Questionnaire (PMSQ). It takes you and the person you are dating or to whom you are engaged through a series of probing, personal questions. The PMSQ provides critical information about your partner's history, philosophy, theology, and life perspective. Information and understanding are some of the best ways to conquer fear, because they reveal the unknown and give insight. Our book *Marital Secrets* includes a copy of this questionnaire.

Courtship must be a time of examination. An extended courtship allows you to view each other when either of you is sick, when one or the other is receiving public recognition, when one is experiencing a crisis, etc. You will find out how well the other person is able to control their appetites and desires as the relationship becomes more physically intimate. If they cannot control themselves before marriage, you know that it will be difficult for them after marriage.

You may ask, "Why should we need to control our desires *after* marriage? After all, isn't it okay then?"

Of course it is. But what if one of you gets sick? For an extended period? What about trips away from each other? What about pregnancy and newborns? If you do not think you will have to exhibit some amount of self-control after you get married, you are sorely mistaken and bound for a huge awakening, if not disappointment.

It is all right if you choose to face up to and accept the other person's deficiencies. But it is *not* all right to get married and then complain about what you don't like, what you didn't know, or what you don't understand about your spouse. If you have an intended spouse or committed partner who recognizes their major deficits and sincerely desires to eliminate them, work with them *before* marriage. You will find out whether changes are long-lasting, acceptable and comfortable for you and the other person. The time frame for correcting the deficits should be determined by the person making the change in their life—not dictated by the other person. However, when you are not married, each party has a free-will choice to stay or to leave the relationship if the time frame for correction becomes cumbersome and too much to bear. If you must end it, be honest, consistent, straightforward and kind with the other person as to why you are terminating the relationship.

If you are not able to accept and tolerate the characteristics, history and future goals of your significant other, then the "But Stronghold" will quickly cause you to negate the promises of change and improvement you perceive. If you see the vision and potential for change and commitment, then strive not to say "but" after your spiritual revelations and knowledge.

The Communication Stronghold

In our clinical practice for the past three decades, we are repeatedly amazed to hear the piercing voice tones spoken by those women who declare that they want to get married. Similarly, we are stunned to hear the threatening and aggressive authoritarian voice tones that spurt from the mouth of those men who assert their desire to find a wife. Neither camp appears to have the insight to recognize the true impact and intensity of their voice on the ear of their receiver. It is often difficult to bear hearing such tones for an hour counseling session, and nearly impossible to imagine one bearing it for fifty to seventy years of marriage. The proper words and message will be lost if not delivered by soothing vocal tones. The speech delivery is just as important as the thought and idea you wish to communicate.

In our recent "Enhancing Romantic Relationship Workshops," we asked single participants to identify their own strongholds and barriers to effective communication. The following were communication strongholds that singles acknowledged they needed to eliminate in communicating with their romantic partners:

1. Poor timing—poor tempo of response when talking with their romantic partner.

2. Misperception of what is meant versus what is being said.

3. Assuming a closed position, or automatically dismissing the person who is speaking in lieu of concentrating on them and their message.

4. Delayed responses to a partner's statements.

5. Fear that shifts to anger while communicating.

6. Feeling afraid that by communicating their true feelings they may get hurt.

7. Being too direct, blunt and frank with opinions.

8. Avoiding conflict by avoiding any discussion of sensitive issues.

9. Being distracted by the movement of the romantic partner while communicating with them.

10. Being bossy and authoritarian with their tone of voice.

11. Unresolved issues that are discussed repeatedly without resolution.

12. Being overly sensitive to the verbal criticism delivered by their romantic partners.

13. Being selfish and self-centered with their communication.

14. Not listening when their romantic partner is communicating.

15. Not being respected and respectful when communicating with romantic partners.

16. Not being talkative and sharing thoughts and feelings that negatively impact the atmosphere in the room.

17. Being too talkative and not allowing the romantic partner an opportunity to be verbally interactive.

18. Wanting the romantic partner to read their mind in lieu of honestly speaking their mind.

19. Two strong-willed people who are not willing to compromise as they communicate.

20. Lack of tolerance for differences.

21. Significant outside influences on personal problems and issues in the relationship, i.e. friends and family members.

22. Not listening to God and being still.

23. Exhibiting defense mechanisms (i.e. projection, rationalization, intellectualization, denial, etc.).

24. Holding a grudge and rehashing numerous past old issues and concerns in the relationship.

25. Allowing children to be present while having unhealthy communications.

26. Forecasting the future of the romantic relationship with unfounded and invalid assumptions and conclusions.

27. Imbalance of money and personal resources.

So what is your communication stronghold and communication style? Would your self-assessment be consistent with the conclusion of your romantic partner, relatives, and friends? Generally speaking, there are four different communication styles; namely:

1. Aggressive—you force your view on your romantic partner.

2. Passive—romantic partner forces their views on you and you become a "follower."

3. Assertive—you negotiate differences with your romantic partner.

4. Passive-Aggressive—you express anger indirectly to your romantic partner.

So which communication style is best in establishing healthy romantic and marital relationships? If you picked #3, you are right.

And which problem-solving style do you practice? There are, generally, three:

1. Flexible—consider a range of alternatives.

2. Rigid—stick only to preconceived ideas.

3. Conciliatory—comply with the demands of your romantic partner without following your own principles or the tenets of your faith.

Which problem-solving style is the best in establishing healthy romantic and marital relationships? Of course, #1 is the best.

For singles to become assertive and flexible in their healthy romantic relationships, they must diligently work daily on several human corrections, but at a minimum they must make a personal commitment not to be:

- Dependent—"people-pleaser"
- Suspicious
- Shy
- Perfectionist—"workaholic"
- Rule breaker
- Egotistical
- Complaining
- Withdrawn
- Anti-social
- Eccentric
- Attention-seeking
- Passive-aggressive
- Avoider of making decisions

We have a workshop for singles entitled "The Midnight Cry: Developing the Character of Wise Maidens and Bridegrooms." During those weekend workshops, and during our psychotherapy sessions with singles, we conduct a unique and powerful skill-building exercise, that we call the "Staying in the Brook" sound exercise. This exercise teaches singles, and others, how to modulate their speech; so that they can manage the intensity of their tone of voice. This skill builder will enable you to modify your voice so that your voice is no greater than the "smoothing" flow of brook water.

We recommend that you secure a sound machine. Learn to set your sound machine volume between four to six on the "brook" setting. Match your speaking voice to the soothing sound of the brook. This effective exercise will gently guide and shepherd your spirit and consciousness to a more relaxed and amendable pattern of speech. This application will eradicate the agitation, anxiety and screeching voice tones that you may be exhibiting. It will extinguish the brassy, coarse and abrasive voice tones that damage communications with your healthy romantic partner.

Proverbs 25:15 instructs us about gentleness and warns us that "through patience a ruler can be persuaded and a gentle tongue can break a bone." Singles, gain control of your tongue and tone of voice for "if anyone considers himself religious and yet does not keep a tight rein on his tongue, he deceives himself and his religion is worthless" (James 1:26).

A gentle voice will chase away stress and create tranquil vocal sounds in romantic relationships. Irritating voice tones will build walls between romantic partners. Choose to speak with your best romantic voice that caresses your friend's ear like the sweet smell of roses that lingers in the room. Let your romantic partner pine for—and thirst for—your voice and your presence, created by the absence of your voice, long after you have left the building. Break the generational curse or stronghold that keeps your voice strident and irritating.

Remember to stay calm, kind and peaceful. Despite the hurtful words you hear from the lips of your romantic partner—stay in the brook. In spite of the frustration you feel with your romantic partner—stay in the brook. In the face of controversy—stay in the brook. Regardless of the momentary fear you may feel—stay in the brook. Remember to never let the devil take you out of the brook. Never let the devil steal your joy, and your peace. Remember to stay in the brook.

Low Frustration Tolerance

During emotional periods of losses, mourning, and grief, it is important to seek balance. You must understand that during peak frustration periods you are likely to make bad choices, poor decisions, and be inclined to take unwise risks causing personal injury to self and others. Conversely, it is important not to allow the other person's frustrations to cause you emotional turmoil. You shouldn't have to get therapy for someone else's problem! Maintaining centeredness in thought, behavior, and actions is critical for self-control. Here are some ways to manage low frustration tolerance:

- Recognize the onset of triggers and symptoms that cause low frustration tolerance.

- Develop a plan of action to manage and eliminate frustration tolerance.

- Implement, and follow through to completion, specific action steps to be taken to achieve and maintain proper frustration management.

- Assess and then evaluate the effectiveness of measures taken to achieve a more desired frustration level.

- Gear your assessment and evaluation process toward specific outcomes that are described and achieved in measurable terms.

Some singles have been searching for a good romantic relationship for years, using the same dating and social methods, and they're not getting what they're looking for. We need to change our methods. John 21:1-7 illustrates that when you fish for a long time and get nothing, you may get frustrated and disappointed. Simon Peter, and his crew kept fishing on the left-hand side of the boat, and kept not getting fish. Fortunately, Simon Peter recognized the voice of Jesus. He told them to cast their nets on the right side of the boat, and their nets couldn't contain the quantity of fish they caught!

When you have a relationship with your Lord and Savior, you have an open spirit to change your past behavior, your past methods, and follow his direction. It is then that you will be able to step into abundant living. When Simon Peter changed his method and followed Jesus' direction to fish on the right-hand side of the boat he was no longer frustrated and was blessed with that in which he sought. Be willing to change your habits and old dating methods that have not successfully yielded the romantic partner that God has for you. What we tolerate, we grow to accept. Grow to not tolerate the status quo if it has not bought you the rich rewards that your heart desires.

Unrealistic View of Adult Life

Life for adults is not about doing what becomes comfortable—it is about doing what is required. We, as adults, far too often know what we want, but we don't know what we need. And what we need is that which is necessary to make us a righteous man or woman of God.

The deeper your roots in the reality of your adult faith, the better you can grow up strong. Our human perception in adult life is not always based on facts. Our perception is marked in specific days, hours and times and clouded by our life experiences, emotions and thoughts. But God lives in seasons, and not in the fraction of our measurement of time. Where we see a period, God sees a comma. The blessing we pray for can still come.

Three Key Issues that Face Singles

1. Singles too often expect romantic partners, family members and peers who don't love themselves to accept and love them.

2. Singles fail to engage themselves in something constructive and progressive.

3. Singles are often in a sporadic or consistent state of anger, opposition, defiance, aggression, destruction, deceitfulness, and/or opposition with those in their home, employment, school, and social environment.

These issues are prominent in our society for several reasons, including but not limited to the following:

- Singles often are victims of physical, sexual, mental, verbal, emotional or psychological abuse. The abuser or one whose attention or love is sought by singles, often will be experiencing frustration, depression, loss of self-esteem, annoyance, threatening behavior or tensions. Statistics consistently instruct us that children who are victims of abuse are likely to grow up to be abusers themselves.

- Often singles feel that their dreams have been beaten out of them as the result of the domestic, social or political abuse they experience.

We believe that there are several approaches for singles to heal and have a realistic view of adult life. Some of the approaches that the single Christian should follow are:

1. Have a zero tolerance for any and all forms of abuse.

2. Establish short, and long range goals.

3. Engage in competitive sports. Sports teach us how to recover and live on after experiencing defeat and failure.

4. Acquire self-empowerment skills through the Word of God.

5. Learn effective problem-solving skills, self-reliance, and good self-esteem and self-concept skills.

Most likely the vision that you have of married life is no more than a fantasy. You may not know how well you have it now in this season of your life.

Today, we want to proudly announce that Nia, Pace and Carol have traveled the fully journey from an unhappy and unholy Christian experience to righteousness and wholeness, according to the will of God. Did you notice that we said "unhappy and unholy Christian?" How can that be?

Understand that, regardless of your level of maturity of faith as an adult always remember that—*there is a devil for your level*. Regardless of your degree of faith, you will always be tempted, tested and tried in your most vulnerable areas. Regardless of your degree of faith, we offer you Jesus who is the source of your hope and your peace. But there is a new character in Christ that you must become if you are to have the victory twenty-four hours a day and all seven days of the week. So to have a holy and unashamed adult life, we encourage you to take a risk and do something with your life that is different from what you have done. In this season of your life take a risk so that God can bless you with abundant living and restore in you what you have lost on this road to adulthood. God wants to reconcile you to him and grant you the desires of your heart in Jesus name.

Nia, Pace and Carol did it. You can too. Let's find out how:

How to Change and Become a New Creature

Bishop T.D. Jakes (Jakes, 2004) instructs us that there are seven (7) steps to a turnaround in our lives; specifically:

> STEP 1: Exposure: Expose yourself to powerful, life-changing options leading you to right decisions and a new perspective.

> STEP 2: Making destiny decisions. Fulfill your God-given destiny by making great decisions based on great information and wisdom from the Lord.

> STEP 3: Transformation: Transform your life by re-newing your mind, freeing it from rigid traditions, and setting you on a new course of victory.

> STEP 4: The tools to build: The right tools to begin building your dreams are the ones God has given only to you.

> STEP 5: The grace to finish: Reject the lies of the devil and finish what God has called you to through His grace and power.

> STEP 6: Receiving your promise: Receive God's promises for your life as a result of your amazing turnaround.

> STEP 7: Positive confession: Be empowered to claim the blessings God is ready to shower upon you by confessing His victories in your life.

I Peter 1: 14-16 tells us that even after you have committed your life to Christ there will be the temptation to backslide and fall back into your old sinful ways. But, we cannot mature in our faith walk and become holy on our own power. We must allow the Holy Spirit to change our personal attitude—our personal spirit—and we must seek the presence of the Holy Spirit. We must allow the power that comes from the Holy Spirit to transform our lives, so that can have the energy and the wisdom we need to resist the devil and to overcome sin. We must gird-up our loins—our foundation in life—and mature in our daily walk of faith.

Further in the eighteenth and nineteenth verses, Peter tells us that the ransom that was paid for our lives was the blood of Jesus. But we should not dare God or threaten him with our lackadaisical decisions and casual disregard for the consequences of our behaviors. The blood of Jesus on this day can wash away all of the sins we have done before this moment. He is a God of second and third chances. The power of the Holy Spirit that Jesus left with us will give each of us a fresh anointing. It will give us boldness, and the courage to make the changes that we need to make in our lives.

When there is a heartfelt conviction there is a chance for a change in our behavior, feelings and thoughts. If you are willing to change, then you don't feel as if the change is difficult or hurtful. But people who have gone through a lot of changes in this world don't quickly wish to change themselves. Those of us who are emotionally tired quickly conclude that we have gone through enough changes already, and now it's someone else's turn to change. But, we should continuously "confess" our sins daily which are done by examining and eliminating the "source of our sin"—the root of the sin—and we cannot just apologize. James 5:16 tells us to confess your faults one to another so that we may be healed.

PERSONAL TESTIMONY

As a young child our aunt, Elsie Bernetta Finner-Howard, would require that before we said our prayers, we had to identify all of our sins and poor judgments of the day. We then were required to identify what alternative behaviors would have been better, and more Christ-like. Aunt Elsie would then require that we confess our sins, repent the motivation in our heart that gave birth to the sin, and make a promise to God that named specifically how we were going to correct any injury that our ungodly behavior had cause others. The daily night prayers would start with praise and worship to

God, and then a prayer of petition; asking God for the strength and wisdom to conduct ourselves more like him. More than fifty years later, this soul cleansing continues to be a nightly practice.

A change in our behavior is not change until there is evidence of the change. And behavior is not changed until it is demonstrated repeatedly and consistently, without relapse, for at least nine to twelve consecutive months. Have you changed? Has your romantic partner changed? Be honest.

So we must be mentally alert, think clearly, and daily quote Corinthians 5:17 that states, "Therefore, if anyone is in Christ, he is a new creation; the old has gone, the new has come!" Peter tells us to be disciplined and exercise self-control. To become mentally strong, and think clearly, we must control and gird-up the loins of our mind, be sober and have hope. An ancient oriental custom was to *gird up* or *tie up* one's loose flowing robes in the process of *getting* ready for hard work. Mature adult life is hard work.

As single Christian men and women we know how to gird up our dress and attire for service in the kingdom of God. We bind and gird up our flesh in girdles in order to fit into our clothing. We gird up our aprons in order to cook. We gird-up many things in our mature adult lives. But as single Christians we must learn how to gird up our tongues, gird up our minds, and gird up our emotions. We need to bridle our daily choices and self-controlled in our behavior so that we can be disciplined, and fulfill our God driven destiny and personal goals. We need to roll up our sleeves, and truly get down to the work and business of living holy. We must be disciplined single Christians in order to be worthy of Jesus's blood.

Before the creation of time and this world our God planned for Jesus Christ to come to the earth and to die on the cross for the redemption of our souls; because all of us have sinned and come short of the glory of God. We come to tell you that Jesus died on the cross for your salvation, and by his precious blood you are saved. If you have confessed your sins with your mouth, and because you have accepted God's plan of salvation for your life, you will live eternally with him in glory. But you must continue to:

- **Sit-up** in your position of responsibility in the body of Jesus Christ so that you can be mentally alert and think clearly.

- **Stand-up** and assume a holy and righteous posture like that of Jesus Christ.

- **Gird-up** for a good fight against the devil that seeks to destroy your spirit with arguments and opposition by unholy romantic relationships.

- **Look-up** and have hope that your daily study of God's Holy Bible, prayer, and faith are healing you from the inside out, so have patience with yourself, your romantic partners, and with others in your life.

Because of your commitment to be holy, and willingness to grow to be more like Jesus each and every day, you are worthy of his precious blood. Sit-up…Stand-up…Gird-up…and Look-up with hope and claim all of your promises and victories under the blood of Jesus, for you are worthy. May the word of God abide in you, strengthen you, create a new creature inside of you, and bring you peace.

WISDOM BOX #3:

1. God holds us responsible for our behaviors just as we hold Him accountable to His covenant with us.

2. An assertive communication style and flexible decision making style will best enhance romantic relationships.

3. Stay in the Brook.

4. What we tolerate we grow to accept.

5. There is a devil for your level regardless of your maturity in God and the strength of your faith.

6. When there is a heartfelt conviction, there is a chance for a change in our behavior.

7. Sit-up, stand-up, gird-up and look-up.

Chapter Five

The Seven Sins of the Single Christian

#1: Excessive Want

We need to examine the spirit of want that we often have as single people. Matthew 6:33 instructs us to "Seek ye first the kingdom of God, and his righteousness; and all these things shall be added unto you." We need to fill our thoughts with the desires of God, we need to take on *His* character for our pattern in life. We need to take on *His* character as our lifestyle, and to serve and obey *Him* in everything. You have to follow the pattern of God *first*—then whatever you ask for will be granted you. God's pattern of living for us is not to want for anything.

Do you have a spirit of want—*that* you want, *what* you want, *how* you want it, and *when* you want it? Is your frustration with not getting what you want, causing you to feel desperate and unfulfilled? Jesus Christ's pattern for us is not to feel desperate, for desperation creates the emotion of depression, and desperation can create delusional thoughts.

But Psalm 23 is clear and direct when it states "The Lord is my shepherd; I **shall not** want." The Life application Study Bible New Living Translation puts it this way: "The Lord is my shepherd; I *have* everything I need." David wrote Psalm 23 from his experience as an earthly shepherd of sheep. The characteristics and pattern of sheep is to be totally dependent on the Shepherd for each and every provision, guidance, and protection. In John 10:11, Hebrews 13:20 and I Peter 5:4 Jesus is referred to as the Good Shepherd, the great Shepherd and the head Shepherd. Sheep are not frightened and passive, but instead they are obedient and wise followers of their Shepherd. We have to have a "made-up-mind" to be a follower—a discipline of the great shepherd Jesus Christ—every hour of every day, and not just when it is most convenient or easy.

So who is your earthly shepherd? Who is your David that provides for you, that guides you, who protects you and who intercedes with God on your behalf? Is your shepherd your pastor, or your friend, or your mother, or your father, or your aunt, or your uncle, or your sister, or your brother, or your woman, or your man? Is their advice and counsel to you consistent with the direction you sense from the Holy Spirit that comes from the core of your heart deep inside of you? Are you confident that what they do and say to you lines up with the holy word of God?

When it comes to yourself, are there visual signs of your total surrender to God, or are there still signs of your living to satisfy your human flesh and lust? Is your lack of total surrender to God the barrier you have created which has prevented God from granting you the desires of your heart? Is your lack of total surrender to God's word the stumbling block to your receiving a righteous romantic partner or spouse? Do you read and know the Word of God?

To eliminate your spirit of want your must first:

- Take on the lifestyle of holiness every day and every hour even in the mist of the lustful, ungodly and unholy urges that overcome your flesh.

- Obey the purpose and mission for our life that will advance of the kingdom of God as set by God and revealed to you through the Holy Spirit.

- Abdicate your free-will to the written Word of God and resign to only do what is there.

- Singles, read the Word of God, work the Word of God, and be blessed with the desires of your heart.

#2: *Emptiness*

Singles experience emptiness on a nearly-continual basis and encounter burdens imposed on them by society's value system. Society and the world pressures singles to enter into a romantic relationship and get married. It is the myth of our culture that eventually everyone will secure a rewarding romantic relationship that is sustained in marriage, with a legacy of children and grandchildren. Needless to say, singles struggle throughout life to achieve their ideal relationships, thereby pleasing themselves and their significant others. Females who are single tend to experience greater personal and social pressure than males who are single. Pressures from peers, family members, and society cause singles tremendous anxiety and emptiness, simply because they have no mate.

Widowers and widows experience emptiness and pain which is somewhat different than divorcees and singles. Emptiness experienced by those who have lost their mates is severe and far too often indefinite in nature; because the loss of a partner by death makes it impossible to replace the feelings provided by a chosen person in their life. They usually need grief counseling or Christian counseling in order to resolve feelings of devastation due to their permanent loss.

What is the first step to resolving emptiness? Self-love. No meaningful relationship can develop without first a real love for self. It is only through self-love that you can share your loved self with another. Once you have established this essential love, you are empowered to lead a full, prayerful life. Those are the catalysts for resolving emptiness, and they will prevent you from filling your emptiness with substitute, but wholly inadequate addictions such as:

- Eating
- Cigarette, cigar, or tobacco pipe smoking
- Caffeinated coffee, soda, or tea drinking
- Gambling—including lotteries, casino activities, house gambling games, and the stock market
- Spending—cash, credit cards, checking accounts, "automatic teller" cards

- Getting involved in any and all sorts of unhealthy relationships
- Unbiblical sexual behavior
- Excessive exercise
- Excessive housework
- Excessive overtime at work

Know that you are not alone. There is an anonymous meeting group for the excessive abuse of each of the above behaviors!

#3: Inappropriate Attractions

As single Christians be mindful of what you draw near to yourself. That will take self-control; Proverbs 25:28 tells us that "a person without self-control is as defenseless as a city with broken-down walls." It will take a recognition that "For all that is in the world, the lust of the flesh, and the lust of the eyes, and the pride of life, is not of the Father, but is of the world" (I John 2:16).

What has always amazed us as clinicians is how those who have been neglected and/or abused by irresponsible, abusive or drug addicted parents or primary care givers are usually attracted to romantic relationships and actually marry persons who also are abusive, neglectful and addicted to drugs. So we find ourselves being drawn to what our eyes—our flesh—are familiar with whether our memories are painful or not.

But as righteous and holy single Christians we must stop doing permanent things with temporary people. Marriage is a permanent thing in God's eye. But most people marry a "concept" and not a "person." That is, most people marry the institution of marriage and not the character of the person. But the Bible tells us to marry one to whom we can be committed for *fifty to seventy years*. The Bible does not tell us to marry solely for attraction and "love."

We should not marry the "man" or the "woman" per se. Instead we should marry the character that extends from the man and from the woman. A person's character is what can be seen and witnessed, and not what is verbally described. The character of a person extends beyond the physical attractive body, just like the rod that extended from the hand of Moses.

Examine yourself. Have you overlooked a good mate match because you are fixed on the familiar? Are you fixed on what has always pleased your flesh in the past—what has previously pleased your eyes—instead of who can enrich your spirit and who can nourish the ministry inside of you? Be open to more options and different profiles of a man or woman while in search of the romantic partner that God has in store for you.

#4: Unhealthy Attachments

As children, we develop personal beliefs and emotional security based on our experience with our primary care takers. Our inner "child self" and sense of attachment to others, generally speaking, is determined by what degree we:

- had a clear understanding and good communication with significant others in our immediate core family environment,

- had someone available to respond to our own personal needs and concerns, and

- had primary caretakers who could abate or eliminate our feelings of helplessness, confusion, instability, rejection, anxiety, frustration and lack of trust in others.

If not evolved, such childhood feelings can lead to adulthood emotional dependence, skepticism and suspiciousness, and we are unable to attach to others in healthy ways.

What is Attachment?

Attachment between two persons in romantic relationships refers to the degree of one's presence and availability to the other when there is a need for fulfillment of love, attention, companionship or problem resolution (Clinton and Sibcy, 2002). An "attachment style is a mental model, a set of basic assumptions, or core beliefs, about yourself and others. Attachment behavior is any behavior that results in persons getting closer in relationships" (Bowlby, 1969).

One psychologist, Kimberly Rene Adams (1999), studied African-American father-daughter relationships and came to some intriguing conclusions. Her results "indicated that, while these young women came from varying backgrounds and family structures inclusive of both informal and formal family styles, there remained a consistent theme that each daughter yearned to be close to her father." For many women, (regardless of race, ethnicity, culture or creed), their ability to establish healthy romantic relationships is directly related to a sense of attachment to the male father figures in their childhood. Single women like Nia often seek "substitute fathers" in their unconscious need to fill the paternal gap in their life. According to Adams, women like Nia often seek romantic partners who can serve as their financial provider, protector, and/or teacher. Interestingly enough, the Adams study indicated that many fathers saw themselves in the first two roles, but not the third. Men have the same challenges, often looking for someone who will meet every need and fulfill every desire.

But men and women were not designed to be anyone's "everything." Ladies, and even gentlemen, your partner must never be your god. Be mindful that it is not wise or fair to expect your romantic partner to be your "god-in-the-flesh" who meets your emotional need for security, protection, direction and provision. Instead, draw near to your spiritual Father—God—for fulfillment of those needs.

#5: Entrapment

It is important to be mindful of the many forms of spiritual bondage and entrapment in romantic relationships. Entrapment occurs most frequently during periods when one is vulnerable, with unmet personal needs. The persistence of unmet needs makes singles vulnerable to being used by others. Instead of looking to have their needs met, they enter unhealthily into relationships where they are used by their partner. There are many reasons for this:

- *Poor self-esteem*—in which singles think and feel less about themselves than how others view them. They feel unworthy and often feel not entitled to things of value that meet their needs.

- *Poor self-image*—in which singles disapprove of themselves, especially their bodies. They feel unattractive and not worthy of the love, attention, or approval they wish to receive from others.

- *Faulty value system*—in which singles feel that what others have materially is far better than what they own. These singles devalue themselves and are devalued by others as a result.

#6: *Abandonment*

Christians run to the church altar and marry far too quickly, often to avoid the entrapment of fornication and sexual sin. The unfortunate consequences are borne out in the rate of divorce among Christians, now estimated at 51%, greater than the divorce rate of 49% among non-Christians (Barna, 2004). Christians, being human, have the same challenges as non-Christians; they find it too difficult to forgive the inevitable irritations, frustrations and offenses that come with marriage.

If you are married, don't be so quick to abandon your gift from God. To counter the risk of abandonment, remember these five secrets:

1. When we are dating often our eyes are closed to the truth about our romantic partner and our heart is open. But after marriage it often appears that our eyes become open and our heart becomes closed. Never let your heart be more open than your eyes.

    You should date at least twelve to eighteen months—every season of the year—before you get engaged. It is difficult to maintain the mere appearance of righteousness and holiness for more than twelve to eighteen months.

2. Don't invest anymore in a person than you are willing to lose. Ask yourself: are you playing the role of wife or husband in the absence of the covenant?" If the answer is yes, then cease and desist from doing those wife- and husband-like things. Question what you have become in order to maintain the relationship. If it is not worth it—if it is not holy and godly—stop it.

3. We can choose our behaviors, but we cannot choose the consequences of our behaviors. Know that you have the God-given power to choose your behavior, feelings and thoughts.

4. In chapter nine, we list the 160 things you need to know about a person before you even think about getting engaged or married. These are issues our divorced clients told us that they wished they had known before the engagement so they would not have had to come to us for a divorce. Know the answers to all 160 questions or be willing to accept whatever is the undisclosed truth for fifty to seventy years.

Abandonment may be intentional or unintentional, but it often leaves the victim defenseless and unable to provide adequately for themselves. If you find yourself abandoned, it is important to remain God-centered at all times and not be distracted by the world from your God-given mission. Matthew 16:26 informs us "For what is a man profited, if he shall gain the whole world, and lose his own soul?" Hold tightly to the teachings of God, the teachings of parents, and lessons learned from previous relationships. Don't allow your emotional needs and fleshly urges in the moment make you defect from the sound bosom knowledge, common sense and wise lessons you have learned.

In order to have healthy romantic relationships, you must make good decisions, use good judgment and be a positive, consistent contributor to this world and to the kingdom of God. You must take care of your own personal needs adequately in order to be capable of providing for the care of others. And you can do it! We are reminded in Philippians 4:13, "I can do all things through Christ which strengthens me." We have seen this proven over and over. Psalm 11:1 and Isaiah 46:9-11 tell us that God's power is not diminished by any turn of events. Hold onto your personal power and faith in God to maintain your hope and empower you to resist fear and temptation.

And remember: though others may, God will never abandon you. "*He* will not fail us nor forsake us" (Deuteronomy 31:6).

#7: *Betrayal*

You don't have to be married to experience betrayal. It is a common source of disturbance and turmoil in singles' lives as well. After they give their love physically, emotionally, and materially, singles who are betrayed feel misused and unappreciated. To make matters worse, the betraying partner on the receiving end feels entitled to the gifts, inflicting permanent damage to the unsuspecting, surprised, and dismayed giver. They assume no responsibility or blame for the hurt and pain, and often render the betrayed giver incapable of establishing future healthy relationships.

Betrayal causes singles to lose faith in themselves as suitable mates for others who may pursue them for meaningful romantic relationships. Betrayal causes singles to abandon personal care of themselves and their needs. The irony of betrayal is that the victim may pursue unhealthy, abusive, and promiscuous relationships, partly because of conditioning and acceptance of past mistreatment. Finally, the ultimate tragedy of betrayal is physical violence, permanent physical damage, or death.

You can cut down your risk of betrayal. Here are a few ways. They're not foolproof, but they'll improve your chances substantially:

- Identify the characteristics that you feel you deserve in a mate or spouse prior to engaging in any relationship considered meaningful.

- Begin the search for a suitable mate or spouse with an open mind, positive attitude, and a spirit of steadfastness.

- Establish a timeframe in which to achieve the pursuit of a suitable mate or spouse you desire, and strictly adhere to established time frames while not allowing any distractions. Decide how long you will invest in a person.

- Continue the pursuit of personal, social, and professional goals while seeking a desired mate or spouse. The development of a spiritual life and becoming God-centered in responding to life endeavors should be foremost in the mind of singles, even during the pursuit of a mate or spouse.

- Once you have found someone about whom you can become serious, begin honest and open conversations which include discussions regarding each person's goals, desires, needs, and expectations. Keep up the dialogue until both of you reach and adhere to mutual agreements.

- After a recommended period of eighteen (18) months of dating, a date should be established for marriage.

- Prior to marriage, professional and Christian counseling is recommended provided by a minister, licensed or certified professional therapist or counselor with specialty in relationship issues.

If, despite your best efforts, you are betrayed, be careful not to lose your true identity and self-respect.

WISDOM BOX #4:

1. Avoid substitute addictions when an unhealthy romantic relationship ends.

2. Stop doing permanent things with temporary people.

3. Only marry who you can make an informed commitment; don't marry someone who you merely "love."

4. Open equally your eyes and your heart, both during courtship and after marriage.

5. Date twelve to eighteen months before engagement.

6. Don't invest anymore in a person than you are willing to lose.

Chapter Six

The Revealing Lesson of the Wizard of Oz

There is a conference, a convention, a workshop for everything from relationships to personal and professional success to communications. Christian conferences of every kind now proliferate.

Are you "conferenced out?" Do you find yourself looking for the spiritual high of a conference to jump-start your motivation to live a changed life?

You're not alone. Many of us are attending an estimated three to seven such conventions, seminars, training sessions and/or personal development workshops each year. Even more of us are receiving counseling or therapy in order to become self-empowered enough to conquer the demands and challenges of our lives. But far too often, we attend such forums in search of answers that we already possess within us. Far too often single people travel down an endless "yellow brick road" in search of the God-given power, authority, emotions, thoughts, motivational gifts and talents that they already possess.

Many of us contend that we are walking in faith, but confess with our mouth that we feel loneliness, emptiness and fear. We publicly testify that we trust in God, but privately acknowledge our lack of wisdom, knowledge, compassion, courage and faith in God's direction for our lives. Many of us close our eyes in total surrender to God as we offer praise and worship, while keeping one eye open, as if to steady our footing down the illusory yellow brick road.

But God has already bestowed upon us free will and every gift, human emotion, attitude and value that is needed to be happy on this day. God has already given you his heart. For we learn that "heart" in the Old Testament is the inner person—the conscious self or personality, with every function (spirit, intellect, emotion, rational thoughts and the free will) that makes a person human.

There is an entertaining analogy between the 1939 classic movie film *The Wizard of Oz*, or the 1978 adaptation, *The Wiz*, to the lifestyle of many single Christian men and women. Let's do a juxtaposition between *The Wizard of Oz* and the faith walk of single Christians and find the intriguing comparisons.

Lyman Frank Baum's 1890s book was adapted for the screen and introduces us to ten-year-old Dorothy Gale who resides on farmland in Kansas with her grounded and no-nonsense Auntie Em and docile Uncle Henry. The role of Dorothy was initially to be played by ten-year-old Shirley Temple instead of the sixteen-year-old Judy Garland. Judy Garland was older, but despite her skills and experience she was cast to perform in an immature and naïve manner inappropriate to her age. If we are honest with ourselves we would acknowledge that we too often exhibit immaturity and a lack of spiritual growth in comparison to the actual number of years that we have been saved by the blood of Jesus Christ. We, like Judy Garland, often are cast in personal and professional "roles" of responsibility that result in our bearing less fruit because of our own spiritual immaturity. But if God has cast you in the role that you now hold then he has already equipped you to perform it with competence, confidence, and grace.

In Kansas, Dorothy and her faithful dog Toto are harassed by Almira Gulch, the rich, powerful, manipulative owner of the majority of farmland in that region of Kansas. She was perceived by Dorothy and her family as being wicked and witching. In protest, despair and fear Dorothy runs away from home. Shortly into her journey she meets a man with the impressive but concocted title of Professor Marvel who tells her exactly what she wants to hear.

Marvels are magicians that create false appearances, fantasies, and dreams that appear to be wonderful, surprising, and amazing.

Marvels create miraculous and supernatural illusions, the figments of one's imaginations. In this life, when we fail to appreciate and content ourselves with our present nourishing environment, twisty troubles and circumstances may move us into making wrong decisions under the undue influence of marvels. Marvels that we meet traveling down the road of life will constraint our free will and overpower us to do those things we would not do if left to act freely. The undue influence of marvels will overcome a lonely, needy or lustful person and make their desires conform to his or her own, obliterating their volition. If the person protests, resents the reality of their single status, or fails to accept their present gift of singleness, they may find themselves caught up like Dorothy in a sudden forward and spinning motion. They often find themselves caught up in unholy sex, immortal conduct, cohabitation or marriage to a marvel that will separate them from home and submerge them in a foreign loveless world called "Oz." Even if your destructive yokes and strongholds are broken there may not be enough time in the midst of your stormy marriage or situation to restore your spiritual peace, sanity, or sense of home without suffering damaging consequences.

Just as Dorothy loses Toto and resigns to facing her responsibilities and challenges, a tornado hits the farmland, she has difficulties returning home and sustains a head injury. Kansas is depicted in drab black and white, while the imaginary Emerald City of Oz to which she is about to go is arrayed in vivid Technicolor.

Isn't that how singles imagine the single versus the married life? The single life is in shades of black, white and gray—dull and lifeless—while the married life is imagined in the same vivid Technicolor as the Emerald City.

And that's the myth. Regardless of our titles, socioeconomic status, or degree of holiness and righteousness, we will always have trials and tribulations.

When you give unto the dark evil feelings of despair, depression, fear and avoidance like Dorothy, you will become vulnerable to the undue influence of those offhanded, perplexed, and hollow persons you meet on the road of life. These ruthless and self-serving "marvels" will create smoke and mirrors to cloud your view and get you off track. With irrational delusions, you are at risk of marrying someone other than God's chosen mate, and your marvelous wedding day will be no more than an illusion.

Often when singles become saved by the blood of Jesus Christ, or are successful in separating themselves from the "marvels" in their lives, they fail to accept the reality that there still will be trials and tribulations. Even when we are successful in denying our flesh, obeying God's will and seeking God's direction for our daily walk of faith, we must accept the black and white Kansas reality that trials and tribulations will be unceasing. Like Auntie Em, single people need to stay focused on the responsibilities at hand, and not flee the beauty of singleness by marrying a "marvel" that they find by chance along the road of life. Singles need to brace themselves for handling each trial and tribulation in life through the empowering grace of God. And they must expect to do that even after they get married.

But you can live an abundant life despite the world's tribulations. As Jesus tells us, "In this world, you will have tribulation. But be of good cheer: I have overcome the world" (John 16:33).

After Dorothy shows maturity by resigning to her reality and appreciating the blessings of her humble Kansas farm life, she finds that her timing is greatly flawed and she can't find her loved ones who give her the meaning of home. Toto escapes from Almira Gulch and reunites with Dorothy, and they seek shelter from the storm in their house that was abandoned by their family. The storm twister dislodges the house with her and Toto in it, which then lands on and kills the Wicked Witch of the East in a magical and enchanted place called the "Land of Oz."

Back to our visual study. In the Land of Oz Dorothy was greeted and helped by the charming Good Witch of the North, Glenda, who came down to earth in a bubble from above. She was also helped by the Munchkins who were playful and silly. The enchanting witch Glenda used her witchcraft and magic to plant the ruby red slippers, worn by the lifeless Wicked Witch of the East, onto Dorothy's feet. The ruby red slippers were the same color as blood, the same color used for Pentecost Sunday, ordinations, fire, energy, and the Holy Spirit (Acts 2:3). Ruby red symbolizes passion and represents one's spiritual enlightenment. Slippers, unlike shoes and boots, are comfortable and can be put-on and off easily like our faith. Glenda told Dorothy that if she would allow the ruby red slippers to be taken off her feet she would no longer be safe from the Wicked Witch of the East.

In a similar way, the yoke of Jesus, the Holy Spirit and our faith are comfortable. They fit. They are the foundation of our Christian life (Matthew 22:28-30). Accepting Jesus Christ as our Lord and Savior at the foot of the cross is the easy part. Rising up and starting your walk of Christian faith is a more difficult daily challenge. The devil wants to destroy our faith walk. Despite all the evil we face by the wickedness of others, we must pray for the strength to stay holy, so that our soul and the quality of our living can be held safe. Just like Dorothy's red slippers, we can not allow marvels and munchkins to cause us to lose our faith and to take us away from holiness, or we will no longer be safe from the wicked people of the world.

*Dorothy wants only to get back to Kansas to her loving family and friends. She is advised **by** the munchkins, the primary inhabitants of this new and unfamiliar territory,, to "follow the yellow brick road," for that will lead to the Wizard of Oz, who will surely know how to get her home. Whenever Dorothy asked the munchkins, "Why should I follow the yellow brick road?" they would simply repeat the mantra, "**Just** follow the yellow brick road."*

The color yellow symbolizes cowardice, jealousy, inconsistency, and adultery. In France the doors of traitors were coated with yellow in medieval pictures. Judas, who portrayed Jesus, was often portrayed in yellow. Interestingly, a meek and soft yellow metallic shade morphs into the color gold. And in the Christian faith, gold is symbolic of our faith. When we take on the meekness, humility and gentleness of Jesus Christ we can transform our cowardice, jealousy, inconsistency, adulterous ways, and wickedness into pure gold. We can overcome all evil cast against us and become successful, consistent Christians (I Peter 2:21-23).

Bricks are composed of a moist compound that has been hardened by heat. Much the same, our attitudes become hard when we are agitated and angered by the unfair actions of others.

Like Dorothy, some singles are blindly walking down the yellow brick road laid in front of them by silly and playful people who neither understand nor explain their rationale. They lack personal discretion, wisdom, faith, and Christian integrity in their daily lives. We must not be a traitor to our faith when we are lonely, frustrated, hurt, or fearful before the great problems of life. At each and every moment, the question to answer is "Whose road am I on now?" We must not walk the hard pathway directed by unwise and silly people; that will only lead to bitterness. We must instead train our spiritual ear to discern a word of direction from the Lord. We must prayerfully seek wisdom and affirmation from the Holy Spirit as to which pathway God would have us follow and not follow the directions of munchkins, whether they are family members, friends, coworkers, neighbors, or romantic partners.

But we digress. One of the most memorable songs in the Wizard of Oz was "Somewhere Over the Rainbow" written by Harold Arlen. Dorothy was looking for a place where there wasn't any trouble. Somewhere over the rainbow "Where troubles melt like lemon drops." She asked the question, "If happy little bluebirds fly over the rainbow, why oh why can't I?"

It is possible to "fly over the rainbow," but only if we have the comfort of the Holy Spirit that Jesus left with us. Through the blood of Jesus we can travel to the other side of our problems and concerns and find joy that empowers us to be Christ-like in our daily lives. Problems may not melt like lemon drops but the power and authority we have under the blood of Jesus will empower us to handle each situation.

Oftentimes, similar to Dorothy's cry, singles ask "If others can get married, God why oh why can't I?" But Dorothy, like most singles, fails to recognize that the bluebirds were first happy as birds and were not trying to become someone or something else. Singles must embrace the concept that the bluebirds were happy first *before* they flew over the rainbow. Singles must grow to be happy with themselves and the life in which they are now planted before they can successfully "fly over the rainbow" into the world of marriage.

Along her travel down the yellow brick road, Dorothy first encounters the Scarecrow made of straw, who, by his own admission, can't scare anyone. The scarecrow had convinced himself that he lacked brainpower. No doubt that being nonproductive by hanging on a field pole in the sun and being subjected to the insults of a crow all day would rightfully lead one to conclude that they lacked good judgment.

Dorothy asked the Scarecrow—"how can you talk without a brain?" He had no explanation. However, when necessary, the scarecrow was skilled at providing directions, originating ideas, and problem-solving. Yet, the Scarecrow wasted his time and energy traveling down the yellow brick road to see the Wizard so that he could give him a brain.

Dorothy next encountered the Tin Man in search of a heart, who only felt good and happy when his joints were oiled. The Tin Man was good at putting out the fire to protect the Scarecrow who was made of straw. Although his exterior presentation was hard, constrictive, and inflexible, he cried easily, and was gentle in his speech and spirit. The Tin Man wasted his best days and enthusiasm joining Dorothy and the Scarecrow in their journey down the yellow brick road to see the Wizard, so that he could be given a heart.

The Lion was self-defeating because he would repeatedly state "I do believe in spooks." His fear allowed the Wicked Witch to dispatch the evil monkeys and capture Dorothy and Toto. But despite his fear, the Lion would physically stand in front of Dorothy and Toto and protect them from the monkeys. Nevertheless, the Lion wasted his strength and glory days in the forest traveling down the yellow brick road to see the Wizard so that he could be given courage.

What we believe we speak, and speaking negatively can release the devil's destructive army against us. Too many of us do not understand that we already have inside us that which we are seeking from someone else. Reflect on how Dorothy had the desire to be home, not realizing that she was already in her comfortable bed at home; for the entire movie was merely her dream. Nonetheless, Dorothy wasted her energy and stamina traveling with the Scarecrow, Tin Man and Lion down the yellow brick road to see the Wizard so that he could help her go home.

When Dorothy, the Lion, the Scarecrow and the Tin Man began along the Yellow Brick Road, they came to a crossroads. They decided to take a shortcut, across a poppy field. Only Dorothy and the Lion were vulnerable to the narcotic effect of the poppy herbs in the field, provided compliments of the Wicked Witch of the East and her playful mischievous monkey sidekick. The poppies were soothing to the eye, but deadly to the spirit.

Poppies, alcohol, marijuana, cocaine, heroine and even other legal stimulants can be soothing for the moment, but life-threatening to our sense of peace, security, self-confidence and boldness in Christ. We must learn not to medicate our uncomfortable feelings and problems with illegal drugs, alcohol, sex, and other self-destructive behaviors. We must not succumb to the spell of wicked mischievous people and artificial happiness. We must hold on to our faith in order to avoid excessive addictive habits, or we will find ourselves, like Dorothy, with a "monkey on our back."

Upon reaching the Wizard, Dorothy and her friends are confronted with the proposition that each of their heart's desires is already within each of them. The Scarecrow always had a brain proven by his good deductive reasoning. The Tin-Man already had a heart shown by his tears that were so bountiful that he could rust. The Lion already had courage demonstrated by his protection of Dorothy and Toto, and Dorothy's desire to go home was merely within her own backyard. She only needed to tap her heels together three times in order to get home.

Much the same, single Christians must grow to realize that they should not need to travel down a "yellow brick road" or motivational assemblies, counseling or therapy in search of their hearts' desires. When we focus our energy and strength on enhancing our walk of faith, improving our holiness and developing our spiritual maturity, we can merely call on the name of the Father, the Son and the Holy Spirit and receive the desires of our heart.

Over the years we have found that successful happy married couples usually find their mate right in their own backyard. Where is the spouse that God would have for you? Are they in your work place? In your social club? On your public service committee? In your church? At your physician's office? Look now!

Remember that there is no place like home. There is no place like feeling at home—at peace—with our Lord and Savior Jesus Christ. Remember that the spouse that God has for you will be nourishing, spiritually matured, and responsible in their role as your spouse. They will not be manipulative, self-serving, wicked or witching. The spouse that God has for you will be open, honest and trustworthy. They will not be false, illusionary, delusional or hollow. The spouse that God has for you will be striking, warm and interesting. They will not be dull and lifeless. The spouse that God has for you will be holy, righteous and capable of handling increasing trials and tribulations in this adult life. They will not be irrational, weak and faithless. The spouse that God has for you will be comforting, flexible and accommodating. They will not be controlling, stormy and adversarial. The spouse that God has for you will be meek, humble, gentle and bold in Christ. They will not be cowardly, jealous, inconsistent and adulterous. The spouse that God has for you will be prayerful, positive and wise. They will not be negative, agitating, angry and unfair. The spouse that God has for you will be peaceful, secure, good and happy. They will not be fearful, addictive, and insecure. The spouse that God has for you will be compatible to you. They will fit your personality like a ruby red slipper, and when with them, you will always feel like home.

WISDOM BOX #5:

1. Expect and be prepared to handle increasing trials and tribulations with grace, knowledge, wisdom and holiness.

2. Bring the degree of spiritual maturity to each situation that is equal to the God-given role into which you have been cast.

3. Do not allow "Professor Marvels" in your life and do not marry marvels, witches, munchkins, or monkeys.

4. Do not allow munchkins to determine which actions and decisions you make.

5. Know who the Marvels, Witches, Munchkins, and Monkeys in your life are and eliminate them.

6. Train your ear to the Holy Spirit and not to the desires of munchkins, marvels, and your flesh.

7. Don't medicate your feelings and problems with drugs, sex or other self-destructive behaviors that will damage your sense of peace, security, self-confidence and holiness.

Chapter Seven

The Quest for Human Touch

Our struggle has been how to have a realistic honest and frank discussion with you about the quest for human touch and sex without being ultra-religious or superficial. The truth of the matter is that all of us have a need for human touch. All touch is not sin. But most sin feels good.

Archibald Hart (1994) puts it simply:

> Women like to touch, but men like to feel. Contrary to what most people think, more men say they have felt forced into unwanted sex either to prove themselves or to comply with peer pressure. Further, men that learn during adolescence how to masturbate to pornography find it difficult to break the habit later. Lust, when uncontrolled, creates many unpleasant situations including inappropriate sexual harassment. Most men think about sex at least several times a day or an hour. Younger men, under age thirty-five, think about it even more often, and the average American male has his first sexual encounter at age fourteen. Interestingly, after age thirty-five the frequency remains about the same. Most young males have their sexual beliefs and attitudes shaped by pornography, and exposure often begins at age thirteen. This distorts their views of how women feel about sex and

what can reasonably be expected from sex, and it sets them up for disappointment in the real world. Real women cannot possibly measure up to the airbrushed, color enhanced, glossy photographs that become the standard of reference for most males.

One complication of premarital sex and sexual promiscuity is that women fail themselves by thinking sex is a sign of commitment and expect that the man will be romantically involved, but they often are not. Women are then guilt-ridden, remorseful and left feeling used. Their guilt feelings often resolve into bitterness, loneliness, loss, emptiness, and frustration. Moreover, because women frequently view sex as a substitute for love, they are flooded in the light of day, with feelings of abandonment, betrayal and hopelessness.

There is a direct relationship between our sinful nature and our sexual choices. We live in a world that has damaged our free-will choice system. This society has confused single Christians relative to what is "good for them" versus what is "desirable." To live holy we should not "obey our thirst for sex and lust," but instead we should subordinate our thirst to our deliberate decision to live righteously. We need to shift our perception and make an empowered lifestyle decision to be ruled by God's written standards.

Easily said, right? Most singles find it difficult to accept the premise that virgins and sexually experienced persons alike can practice sexual abstinence and not go blind or die from the "phantom genital pain." But you can be celibate and practice sexual abstinence only after having a heartfelt commitment to do so. You have to literally and consciously decide not to think about sex, touch and lust for a romantic partner. Can you?

Galatians 5:16 tells us, "This I say then, walk in the spirit, and ye shall not fulfill the lust of the flesh." Romans 13:14 and Titus 2:11-12 confirm that success over controlling your sinful nature, lust and thirst for physical touch can only be achieved when you learn to literally shift your thoughts towards godliness so that your feelings can follow. Shift your thoughts to subjects that will abate, replace, and help you avoid the sexual thought or temptation, and then sustain that concentration. Set boundaries with romantic partners and establish a realistic agreement relative to touching, feeling and sex by the third date. Establish a specific escape plan for every possible situation. Know what your personal sexual triggers are and avoid them at all cost. Imagine the negative feelings, guilt and remorse you will experience if you violate your body in this way (see I Corinthians 6:18) and avoid that damage to your spirit beforehand. Stay in public places and do only what you would do in front of Jesus Christ. You might even want to ask a spiritually mature friend to hold you accountable by agreeing to listen to you when you are in crisis or have fallen, to help you stay—or get back—on track.

We must refrain from using the mercy and grace of God to excuse habitual sin. We must work each day to resist the devil just a little more than we did the previous day. We must recognize that the devil uses tangible things to satisfy our physical needs, but our Father God uses spiritual weapons to sustain us and to bring us peace, and that those spiritual weapons are stronger than the physical weapons arrayed against us. As Paul reminds us, "…the weapons of our warfare are not physical, but mighty through God to the pulling down of strongholds…" (Corinthians 10:4).

Every single has something that they do that brings an adrenaline rush, that power and energy that causes one's blood to flow and climaxes in a gratifying endorphin high. Adrenaline rushes are either emotionally or physically based, and sex is of course one of the ways that God has created to bring on that rush. But it's not the only way. If you were physically disabled and a wheelchair bound quadriplegic, what would you do? There are other adrenaline rushes that will honor our Lord, while giving us energy and a gratifying climate of joy, peace and glory.

Effective Strategies for Sexual Relapse Prevention

Fornication is defined on three levels; specifically:

- Sexual intercourse other than between a man and his wife, or
- Sexual intercourse between a spouse and an unmarried person, or
- Sexual intercourse between unmarried people.

Singles are usually sexually tempted into fornication through their:

1. Dreams

2. Feelings

3. Memories

4. Conversations

5. Physical "thing" reminders (i.e. the bed, underwear, clothing, etc.).

6. Physical "people" reminders (i.e. former spouses and lovers).

7. Physical "place" reminders (i.e. a former lover's house, motel, automobile, etc.)

8. Music

9. Movies

Psalm 46 tells us that God is our refuge and strength a very present help in trouble. As you grow and develop your faith walk, try these behaviors when your flesh is tempted to fornicate:

1. Find distractions/activities interesting enough to keep you from following through with the sexual temptation.

2. Talk to someone of the same gender as you about anything other than relationships, romance and sex.

3. Talk to your Christian mentor or elder to which you have agreed to be accountable.

4. Think of the negative spiritual consequences of having sex. Feel the guilt now before having sex and not after the sexual act.

5. Immediately seek and attend a church service (i.e. Bible study, prayer meeting, choir rehearsal, etc.).

6. Think of positive consequences of not having sex and congratulate yourself for being faithful to God.

7. Go to sleep—alone.

8. Use relaxation techniques, massage, exercise, pray, be still and know that God is in control.

9. Read the Bible and religious literature in a serene and quiet place.

10. Do positive self-talk out loud that reinforces the benefits of avoiding sexual intercourse now.

11. Sing a hymn or gospel out loud.

12. Leave the situation and get into a safe place. Similar to those who are recovering from drugs—remember no wet places and no wet faces. You must protect yourself by not allowing yourself to be in places that could reasonably result in your having sex (i.e. bedrooms, private residences late at night, etc.)

All right. We hope that this good wisdom and advice isn't going into one ear and out of the other. If you sincerely wish to consistently and successfully live a holy life, then you must have a plan in place before you feel lonely and are tempted by a wet face or a wet space. Be stern, empowered and strong.

WISDOM BOX #6:

1. Strive for emotional adrenaline rushes instead of physical adrenaline rushes for a gratifying endorphin high.

2. Don't just marry a professing Christian, whose lifestyle and personality are not compatible with your own.

Chapter Eight

How to Achieve a Godly Hook-up

In our clinical practice for the past three decades, we have asked many successful married couples how they met their spouse. We have compiled a list of how their godly "hook-up" occurred. You are strongly encouraged to try these methods:

- Airport / on the airplane
- Ballroom dance classes
- Bank lobby
- Bingo games
- Bookstores
- Certified Public Accountant Offices
- Church ministries or activities, such as picnics, banquets, cultural art events, occasions that are open to the public
- Classmates
- Concert Halls
- Dance Lessons
- College/Universities
- In the workplace

- Libraries
- Music lessons
- Organizational/political meetings or events
- Physical fitness centers
- Private home parties
- Professional In-Service and Mandatory Training Courses
- Public policy forums
- School Reunions
- Skating Arena
- Sports Arena
- Study groups at school
- Supermarket/Grocery Store
- Through relatives
- Through beautician, hair stylist, barbers, manicurist, masseuse, braider, cosmetologist, tailor, etc.
- Through Christian friends
- Through coworkers
- Through neighbors
- Restaurants

Do you want to date? Let your family members, friends, and acquaintances know! There are some important blessings that will not come knocking at the front door of your home: a career, a job and a holy romantic partner. Approach finding a good romantic partner like finding a good paying professional job in the downtown high rent district. Let's go!

Equally Yoked, But Not Equally Matched

Far too often people of faith make the mistake of believing that being equally yoked with their romantic partner is merely marrying someone of their own faith. Paul is clear when he teaches us in Corinthians 6:14-18 (NLT):

Don't team up with those who are unbelievers. How can goodness be a partner with wickedness? How can light live with darkness? What harmony can there be between Christ and the Devil? How can a believer be a partner with an unbeliever? And what union can there be between God's temple and idols? For we are the temple of the living God. As God said:

"I will live in them
and walk among them
I will be their God,
And they will be my people.
Therefore, come out from them
And separate yourselves from them, says the Lord.
Don't touch their filthy things,
And I will welcome you.
And I will be your Father,
And you will be my sons and daughters,
Says the Lord Almighty."

But people of the same faith can worship and praise the Lord together in the church house, then leave the church building, go home and then fail to have a lifestyle together that is compatible and happy. Each person can have two completely different lifestyles that both honor and reverence God. One may enjoy their music loud while the other enjoys soft tones. One may be a night owl, while the other is demonstrative and energetic. They both love the Lord and keep his commandments, but can't bear living with their incompatible differences each day. If you are equally yoked by faith, the question then becomes, *does the person's benefit to me outweigh the irritating behaviors that I know about this person and the obnoxious conduct that I have witnessed? Am I able to keep my eyes on resolving the struggle that comes from the principalities, instead of getting hangup in our respective personalities?* Be wise; don't just marry a "faithfellow," but be sure to marry someone in the faith that is compatible with your lifestyle and personality. Both goals must be achieved in order to be happy and content.

The Lesson of the Ox and the Donkey

Although both animals are pack animals, there is an important lesson for singles to learn about oxen and donkeys.

An ox is known for their endurance and relentless energy. They are persistent, tireless, and faithful to each task, responsibility, and heavy load placed on their back. An ox goad is a pointed stick used to urge the ox to further an effort. Oxen are flexible and more acceptable to guidance and direction by the master's ox goad (Imagine this!). Similar to (some) human beings, oxen are self-empowered, assertive, and give generously of themselves. Oxen are respected for their enormous physical and mental strength and stamina during each challenge. They are devoted, positive, and teachable. Like (some) humans, oxen are goal-directed, hardworking, and reverent. Oxen are survivors regardless of what load—what challenge or problem—that their master places on their back.

However, donkeys are quite different. A donkey is more sure-footed on mountain roads, and is bred and naturally suited to carry cargo. But donkeys resist to fulfilling their natural purpose. Donkeys will sit down and abandon a task at will. Donkeys are inherently stubborn, rigid, unpredictable and inflexible. Like (some) humans, donkeys are non-supportive, guarded, lazy, selfish and lack affection. Donkeys fail to show intimacy, concern or tolerance. Like (some) humans, donkeys are easily discouraged when problems arise, and lack responsibility. Donkeys have a conflict-driven avoidant nature, negative attitude, and lack progressive goals. Donkeys refuse to move, are self-centered, procrastinate and cause others to be late. Like (some) humans, donkeys are controlling, noncommittal and unfaithful.

Deuteronomy 22:10 tells us "Do not plow with an ox and a donkey harnessed together." An ox is larger and stronger than a donkey, and because of their differences in size and strength, they cannot pull a plow evenly together. This passage is illustrative and teaches us that an ox and donkey cannot be harnessed and plow together in the same field, because their characteristics are different. *Singles, you can't be a strong ox in the kingdom of God and hang out with a donkey. You can't be an ox and hang out with an ass* if you want a happy and prosperous life. What we tolerate in our personal lives we grow to accept. But as righteous and holy single Christians we must stop doing permanent things with temporary people.

Genesis 2:18 says "And the Lord God said, "It is not good for the man to be alone. I will make a companion who will help him." Companionship is fellowship. The word of God does not proclaim that every man and every woman are to be under the covenant of a legal marriage. All singles are not appropriate for marriage. Be wise and let donkeys remain single and oxen marry each other. Thus, your co-laboring together in the field of life will yield a field of good crops and an abundant life.

The "Sport" of Dating

Modern dating, as we know it, has only been around for about 100 years. This social and recreational dating can serve a number of purposes: stress relief, social intercourse, immediate gratification, and sometimes even privileges usually limited to marriage, albeit without the responsibilities. It is characterized by superficial discussions about school or jobs, problems in the work place, activities of the week, hobbies and relationships with others. It is only infrequently that couples involved in this kind of superficial dating will discuss their personal history and struggles, spiritual strongholds, weaknesses, fears, insecurities, inadequacies and worries. Tragic and irreconcilable marital discord is too often the result of failure to discover this information during the dating stage.

Let's compare dating to thoroughbred horse racing, considered by most horse owners and trainers to be the premier form of racing. Horse races are full of excitement. The colors, the sounds, the smells and the suspense combine to make palms sweat and hearts race. Some races have high stakes that attract many of the nation's finest horses and therefore increase the wagering, sometimes to an all-time high. While wagering and attendance may remain strong, they often fall after a thoroughbred's initial year of racing.

Faithful racing fans usually maintain their strong support of thoroughbred horses even when they face stiff competition. They appreciate the horse's quality, they like the prestige, and they enjoy the "perks" that go with being supportive fans. The dollars they provide attract top stables and horses.

Breeders raise horses, owners race them, trainers train them, riders ride them and fans bet on them to win. Some horses successfully establish themselves as top grass horses and some have fewer victories. Horses that have been defeated can come back to win over better-known thoroughbreds.

As a spectator and player, it is most important to identify and evaluate each horse, then decide whether you think they will "win," "place," or "show."

Let's now look to the kinds of dating that one can engage in. Then you'll be able to decide where your date fits.

"Pleasure Dating" occurs in the initial months of the relationship. It cannot sustain over the long-term. In fact, if it does, the inevitable result is trouble.

In the "Pleasure Dating" phase, the individuals are easily excited and aroused by the outward appearance of each other. We far too often rush to judge that a Pleasure Date is "the one." We then tell our friends and relatives exaggerated truths and fantasies about this new "special person." This emotional activity enhances our senses, causing us to become romantically delusional, deaf to the truth, blind to the obvious and racing at full speed toward a wedding altar built on sinking sand. Pleasure Daters often rush toward marriage with inadequate information and without a solid foundation.

If a Pleasure Date's worthiness doesn't increase with time the superficiality and good façade will wither away after the initial twelve to eighteen months of dating. Life experiences and wisdom teach us that it is difficult to maintain a false appearance of righteousness and sincerity for more than twelve to eighteen months.

One partner involved in the Pleasure Dating phase may be faithful, committed and a strong support of the other person even in the face of competition in the dating race. They will give privileges better limited to a more serious relationship. Unfortunately, this one committed Pleasure Dater may attract others who are better at receiving than giving, handicapping the dating race to the receiver's advantage.

Before giving out privileges, it is important to discover the answers to questions like: How was this person raised? What would friends, former romantic partners, even former spouses say about this person? Who are their peers, mentors, and intimate friends? Who are the people they aspire to emulate? Are they dating anyone else right now? Do they want to?

And before these questions are answered, it is important to set "revocable boundaries." Some people are great friends to spend time with watching television at home. Others love to go out to restaurants or formal events. Still others are great for sports or fitness activities. However, none of these people will necessarily advance to the "winner" category. Until you spend significant time finding out about a person and their background, it is important not to send the wrong signals to a "place" or "show" dating relationship.

The trials of dating will test your trust and belief in your date. The trials of dating will allow you to ascertain the person's quality, value and character. I Peter 1:7 tells us about the test of our faith. The trials of dating are to test your faith in the relationship and to demonstrate if the relationship is strong and pure. The dating process is a test—just like fire tests and purifies gold.

If your faith in the person remains strong after being tried by the fires of dating, it will bring you much joy, assurance and honor if God reveals that you should marry. I John 4:1 (NLT) tells us "Dear friends, do not believe everyone who claims to speak by the spirit. You must test them to see if the spirit they have comes from God." Many of you may unknowingly be in a losing situation with the person whom you are dating. But you must understand that it takes a spiritual test—and testimony—to get a winning marital attitude.

The Security of Courting

Courting differs from dating in that it seeks bosom knowledge and intimacy. In comparison, dating tends to follow principles of competition and contest like a horse race. Courtship was honored prior to the twenty-first century; it required a more thorough, in-depth and itemized study of each other and the two families involved. The investigation would allow both individuals to make secure, competent and informed decisions whether to invest in each other and each other's families. The decision to further invest in the person also would involve making a commitment to support that person's intimate walk with their God, a commitment to their purpose and mission in life, and a commitment to the spiritual calling on their life. Such a complete investigation would not be perceived as intrusive, but would honor the personal value, relevance and standing that the person held in the life of their beloved. In the biblical model, courtship usually occurs once in a lifetime, and the ultimate goal is a binding lifelong covenant marriage. The biblical model of courtship is limited only to those persons viewed as having a "winner" standing.

Biblical courtship or marital commitment is the outgrowth of one's free will that is manifested in an informed, intellectual, emotional, and God-led decision to engage in a covenant promise and a trusting relationship with another. This is the best form of dating. A biblical marital commitment or covenant has certain rights, privileges, duties and obligations, and is binding. The unfortunate reality, however, is that far too many married persons who fail to successfully complete investment and investigative dating tend to maintain a single lifestyle. Despite their marital status, many of them have been bound by a "fear-to-commit" stronghold.

The Lesson of the Three Wells

The ancient stories of scripture are so interesting, but most of us breeze by those familiar passages without digging into their meaning. Let's look at one that talks about "digging," then "dig" into it ourselves to get something of value to take away.

Genesis 26:12-23—The passage tells us that Isaac dug two wells and the herdsmen of Gerar filled them with dirt. The New Living Translation tells us that the first well was named "Argument" because the herdsmen argued about it. The second well was named "Opposition" because there was a fight over it. And Isaac exercised discipline and self-control when he abandoned both the first and the second well, traveling onward to dig the third well, and the local people finally left him alone. So Isaac called it "Room Enough," because he believed at last the Lord had made room for them, and they would be able to thrive.

Throughout the scriptures we find that "well water" represents our spirit. It is important to be mindful that people will put dirt, gossip, abuse, and pain in your wells (in your spirit) and directly or indirectly stop the living water in you. They will try to hinder your spirit with their *argumentative* and *oppositional* nature.

But learn how to end toxic and ungodly relationships and do what Isaac did by going from well to well—from blessing to blessing—without looking back. Until you can separate yourself from the masses in holiness, the Word of God cannot work in your life. You must be willing to let go of the dirt and sin in your life and start anew. And then God will direct you to *your* final well…to *your* awesome blessing…to *your* husband…to *your* wife…to *your* career…to *your* ministry in his kingdom where *you* can thrive without arguments and opposition.

How to End Toxic and Unhealthy Relationships

We can't say this enough: we *must* stop doing permanent things with temporary people. To end and bring closure to an unproductive, un-heavenly, or just plain bad romantic relationship that you know is not from God means to have a finished conclusion or reach the end. It does not mean to transform the relationship to another level and then continue onward. The danger is that such a transformation is illusionary; because some of the emotional elements in the intimate relationship must continue to live in the so-called "transformed" relationship. The great risk is that the mere existence of the old emotional elements will be the trigger to the other suppressed emotions. Any "social occasion" will serve as the bond that can revive the old spark and will usher in ungodly behaviors such as adultery or infidelity. We place security bars and alarm systems around our homes and in our automobiles. We need to place safeguards around our single lives. Safeguard your faith by ending and dismissing toxic and unhealthy relationships.

When you end a romantic relationship, learn how to separate yourself. Do not disrespect your former romantic friend's or spouse's genuine loss and deterred dreams by showing them pictures of your new romantic partner—their replacement. Don't expect calls from the dead. When the relationship is over, place it among dead things, not to be resurrected.

So you ask, "How do I leave a lover or a romantic partner?" Here are some suggestions and strategies:

1. Have a face-to-face discussion as to why you are ending the relationship. Plan your statement, delivery and exit without allocating any of your power to your friend.

2. Create and mail a video message with your decision and eliminate any blame-shifting.

3. Write them a good-bye letter explaining your decision and requesting that they not communicate with you any further.

4. Refuse to return telephone calls, e-mails, text messages, letters, etc.

5. Arrange a meeting in a public place in order to deliver your decision. Control the situation, your message, and exit from the scene.

6. Orchestrate a temporary separation (i.e. three to six months) in order to readdress the validity of your decision to end the romantic relationship.

7. Consult with wise relatives and friends of your romantic partner who are knowledgeable of their reactions in order to learn the best way to end the relationship. Be careful here, and only talk to individuals who you can trust to keep your confidence.

If You Decide not to Leave, or Want to Rethink Your Decision…

Engage in open and meaningful discussions of the issues that cause conflict and confusion. Attempt to identify issues that can be resolved and begin discussions of each item and attempt to reach an understanding and compromise. Seek professional counseling for troubling and problematic issues rather than consulting friends and others who are not able to provide needed understanding and solutions for issues that exist. You may need medication and professional help to manage stress and anxiety related to in toxic relationship turmoil. Ultimately, seek God for development of inner strength and faith building. Spiritual healing is often necessary for resolution of toxic relationships.

All persons involved in toxic relationships should seek professional and spiritual help together. This is important to emphasize because counseling can teach valuable lessons, impart wisdom, and give perspective.

How to End Ungodly Engagements

It is far more embarrassing to face a public divorce in open court in front of fifty to sixty strangers than it is to cancel a wedding that was not ordained by God. It is more sensible to lose an estimated $10,000.00 for a single day of superficial celebration than be miserable for three to ten years and then pay another $5,000.00–$10,000.00 for a divorce. It is preferable to assume the peaceful responsibility for personal debts for the cost of a canceled wedding than share marital debts with an adversary during a divorce. Swallow your pride, cancel all of the wedding plans, cancel all contractual services, pray, be still, and draw near to God. If you have serious doubts, do it now!

Also, wherever you are in your relationship, take the Finner-Williams Pre-Marital Screening Questionnaire (PMSQ) located in Chapter Nine. If your FDAA score is less than 360, then, with the love and support of your family members and friends, complete the following steps immediately:

- Give closure and termination notice to your intended spouse by one of the means discussed in the previous section.

- Match the level of wedding cancellation notification to the same level of the announcement. For example, if the wedding announcement was informal and verbal, then the cancellation notification should be the same. If there was a printed or engraved wedding announcement, then the cancellation notification should be printed or engraved.

- If the wedding cancellation notification is less then three weeks or twenty-one days, then person-to-person aggressive efforts must be made by verbal word, telephone, electronic-mail, and carrier service. This should be followed by a printed or hand-written wedding cancellation notification, by whoever is hosting the wedding. The host may be the parents of the bride, the bride or the couple themselves.

- The wedding cancellation notification should read:

     Mr. and Mrs. John Doe
     announce that the marriage of their daughter
     Mary Jane Doe to Mr. Able Body Chad
     has been cancelled.

- Within thirty days, the bride should return the engagement ring to the groom and the wedding presents to the guest. Yes, ladies, return the engagement ring, cancel the intent to covenant with each other, and plan to start a new life. We pray for your wisdom, discernment, boldness and strength.

WISDOM BOX #7:

1. ***You can't be an ox and hang out with an ass.***

2. What we tolerate in our personal lives we grow to accept.

3. When the relationship is dead, place it among dead things. Do not make attempts to resurrect.

Chapter Nine

Employing Methods of Investigation

Once upon a time, dating and getting married was easy. You met someone from within your community, probably went to the same schools, the same church. You knew their family; they knew yours. There were few questions. Roles were simple and clear.

How things have changed! The person you meet who may be "the one" may not have grown up in the same area of the country or world as you. You may need to employ a private detective, matrimonial attorney, and utilize available criminal and civic computerized Internet clearing house systems to discover the truth about their family history or personal background.

What does this mean for dating today? It means that quality relationships will have to include candid and respectful communication—communication that involves going beyond the basic facts to full disclosure, honesty, truth and a sincere commitment to continually improve interactions and understanding.

Who knows? Maybe it's better this way. Marital discord often occurs because during the courtship each spouse fails to complete an *itemized study* of their intended partner. That may sound cold, but it is one reason couples are guarded and are not equipped to resolve the issues in their marriage from a solid position of *knowledge, tolerance and acceptance.*

Information is no more than the mere gathering of facts and details, with no guarantee that such news is valid. Possessing such information places one in a position to "learn the truth" through conducting further research and investigating those gathering facts. Information leads to learning. Learning brings about knowledge. Having knowledge about a romantic partner means to experience and associate yourself with them to the degree that you become aware of, acquainted with, and intimately familiar with every aspect of their life. Having *"bosom knowledge"* about a romantic partner means that you have relevant, adequate and verifiable information about them that results in your best understanding, comprehension, and wisdom.

Tolerance means having knowledge about unfavorable information, practices, conditions, attitudes, and behaviors about your intended partner that you can recognize, respect and not complain about. *Tolerance* means, although you have *"bosom knowledge"* about that negative aspect of their life, you can allow your partner the freedom to behave in that manner. It is important to recognize and accept that what is merely tolerated today may lead to anger, hurt, frustration, and fear tomorrow. What is tolerated today will lead to a consistent point of contention and argument in the near future.

And finally, *acceptance* is the cognitive process of reaching the conclusion that something is adequate or "right enough" to satisfy your own personal need, to satisfy your inquiry, or is consistent with your standard of living. *Acceptance* of any aspect of your intended partner's life is reaching a decision that their practices, conditions, attitudes, and behaviors are proper or right from your perspective.

An in-depth premarital study should be exhaustive, revealing the impact of personal history on each partner's makeup, belief systems and behavior. The history includes, at a minimum, significant life events, family interactions, personality, major life incidents, past traumatic experiences, thoughts, feelings, emotions and behavior, as well as morals, values, beliefs, spirit, soul and faith. A lack of "bosom knowledge" about your intended will lead to feelings of frustration, anger, bewilderment and a litany of questions.

The exhaustive revealing of personal and family histories before the engagement period can provide an explanation for the behavior patterns, thoughts and feelings spouses display *after* the wedding. Full and honest discovery during courtship and dating can reveal a probable answer to the multitude of questions that arise when one is hurt, fearful, frustrated, angry, bewildered, and pondering endlessly a litany of questions and concerns of the heart that often begin with "why did you do that?" It is crucial during your periods of dating, courtship and engagement, that you "know what you know and how you came to know it."

Here's a tool that can help. The Finner-Williams Pre-Marital Screening Questionnaire (PMSQ) is made up 160 questions that let you know how familiar you are with your partner. The questions are based on a combined total of more than sixty years of counseling and legal experience. We questioned numerous individuals about what it was they failed to know about their partner or spouse which led to marital discord, separation, and/or divorce.

It may be beneficial to retake this screening test every three to four months, after an initial three months of dating, to determine if you are getting better acquainted with each other or becoming stagnant in the Pleasure Dating stage. If you answer it honestly, you will know whether you are "Pleasure Dating," "Investment Dating," or in the phase we call "Biblical Courtship."

By now you may be saying, "How unromantic, crude and impersonal!" To you we say, "So is divorce." This screening survey will assist you with determining whether you know enough about the person you are considering marrying and whether you can accept their issues and inadequacies. Be wise and **do not rush to conclusions about the relevancy that a dating partner should have in your life. Observe a person's behavior throughout the four seasons of a year to learn how they handle a full array of life circumstances.**

THE FINNER-WILLIAMS
PRE-MARITAL SCREENING QUESTIONNAIRE
(PMSQ)

INSTRUCTIONS: This questionnaire consists of six groups of statements. Please read each group of statements carefully. Please read each rating statement across the top and then pick out the one rating statement for each information item that best describes your level of "bosom knowledge, tolerance and acceptance." Circle the number across from the information item you have picked. Only chose one rating for each information item. If more than one rating for an information item seems to apply equally well, circle the lowest number. Be sure that you do not choose more than one rating for each information item.

There are 160 information items located in the first vertical column. The four rating statements are listed horizontally across the top and are as follows:

Column	Rating Value	Rating Statement
A	0 =	No "bosom knowledge"
B	1 =	"Bosom knowledge" that is not acceptable
C	2 =	"Bosom knowledge" that can be tolerated for 50-70 years
D	3 =	"Bosom knowledge" that is accepted or this item is not applicable

SCORING: The PMSQ is scored by summing the ratings for the following sections:

Section 1 =	36	items for months 1-3
Section 2 =	20	items for months 4-6
Section 3 =	30	items for months 7-9
Section 4 =	33	items for months 10-12
Section 5 =	25	items for months 13-15
Section 6 =	16	items for months 16-18

Total 160 items

Each item is rated on a four-point scale ranging from 0 to 3. Circle your honest rating (i.e. 0, 1, 2, or 3) for each information item. Determine your sub-totals for each of the four columns at the end of each center. Then determine the final sub-total for each section. Find your Full Disclosure and Acceptance (FDAA) Score by following the simple mathematical procedures at the end of the questionnaire. The FDAA total score is the sum of the ratings given in boxes A, B, C, and D on all 160 items. There are six sub-total scores for A, B, C, and D that are totaled at the end.

This screening process is intended to be used when someone has determined that their partner is a "Winner." *The time frames associated with the various topics are advisory, flexible and informal guidelines.* The order should be determined by what issues are most important to the individual who is engaged in the Investment Dating process. Feel free to use your own personal language and words if necessary, as long as they parallel the concepts listed. It is our professional opinion and personal belief that, in most situations, a couple should date a minimum of twelve to eighteen months *before* discussing the possibility of becoming engaged to marry. Also, it is our contention that if you do not know and accept the answers to a majority of the following questions and their sub-parts, then it is not time to become engaged and/or married. Try to cover at least two to three areas each month. May God bless you with wisdom, discernment, self-empowerment, grace, compassion and mercy as undertake this journey.

INFORMATION ITEMS	RATING STATEMENTS			
MONTHS **1-3** OF **DATING**	A. No bosom knowl-edge	B. Bosom knowl-edge that is not accept-able	C. Bosom knowl-edge that can be tolerated	D. Bosom knowledge that is accepted or not applicable
Do you know the full name of the person you have been dating?	0	1	2	3
Have they ever been known by any other name(s)?	0	1	2	3
What history does the person have of physical, medical, mental and emotional prob-lems; developmental delays; allergies; learning disorders; alcohol or substance abuse?	0	1	2	3
How much "speed dating" have they done?	0	1	2	3
Have they been gainfully em-ployed for at least 8 hours a day, for 5-7 days a week within the past month?	0	1	2	3
Where are they currently employed?	0	1	2	3
On a typical day, how much do they use alcohol, mari-juana, cocaine, heroin and/or cigarettes?	0	1	2	3
How much education did they complete?	0	1	2	3

INFORMATION ITEMS	RATING STATEMENTS			
MONTHS **1-3** OF **DATING**	A. No bosom knowledge	B. Bosom knowledge that is not acceptable	C. Bosom knowledge that can be tolerated	D. Bosom knowledge that is accepted or not applicable
When did they earn their high school diploma or GED?	0	1	2	3
How many college/community college years/credits do they have?	0	1	2	3
What is/was their college major?	0	1	2	3
What is/was their GPA?	0	1	2	3
Why did they drop out of school/college?	0	1	2	3
When attending school, were they in regular classes or special education?	0	1	2	3
How many times were they suspended in school and for what reason?	0	1	2	3
How many times?	0	1	2	3
What is their current marital status?	0	1	2	3
How many sons, daughters, foster children, stepsons, adopted sons, step and/or adopted daughters do they have?	0	1	2	3

INFORMATION ITEMS	RATING STATEMENTS			
MONTHS **1-3** OF **DATING**	A. No bosom knowledge	B. Bosom knowledge that is not acceptable	C. Bosom knowledge that can be tolerated	D. Bosom knowledge that is accepted or not applicable
How did they personally contribute to the failure of the marriage(s)?	0	1	2	3
Have they ever been in the military service?	0	1	2	3
If so, what branch of the military?	0	1	2	3
When were they discharged from the military?	0	1	2	3
Are they in the military reserves? What was their rank at discharge? What was their discharge status?	0	1	2	3
Do you have flashbacks associated with their military service?	0	1	2	3
What educational experiences did the person's parents receive?	0	1	2	3
What are/were the occupations of the person's parents?	0	1	2	3
How old were the person's parents when he or she was born?	0	1	2	3

INFORMATION ITEMS	RATING STATEMENTS			
MONTHS **1-3** **OF DATING**	A. No bosom knowledge	B. Bosom knowledge that is not acceptable	C. Bosom knowledge that can be tolerated	D. Bosom knowledge that is accepted or not applicable
What is the ethnic background of their parents and maternal/paternal grandparents?	0	1	2	3
Is the person homosexual, heterosexual or bisexual?	0	1	2	3
Have they kissed or rubbed genitals with a female (for females)?	0	1	2	3
Have they been living on the down-low (DL) (for males)?	0	1	2	3
Have they had any sexually transmitted diseases and if yes which ones?	0	1	2	3
Have you ever observed or participated in a *ménage-a-trois* (threesome)?	0	1	2	3
What is the quality of their dress style, grooming skills, personal appearance and personal/oral hygiene?	0	1	2	3
SUB-TOTAL for months 1-3 (36 items):	#:	#:	#:	#:
1. SUB-TOTAL SCORE: _____				

INFORMATION ITEMS	RATING STATEMENTS			
MONTHS **4-6** OF **DATING**	A. No bosom knowledge	B. Bosom knowledge that is not acceptable	C. Bosom knowledge that can be tolerated	D. Bosom knowledge that is accepted or not applicable
Whom does the person live with and is this permanent?	0	1	2	3
How clean do/did their parents keep their home(s)?	0	1	2	3
How many times have they been held at the juvenile detention facility, local police precinct, booked into a county jail, or incarcerated in prison?	0	1	2	3
What were the charges for each?	0	1	2	3
Are they currently on probation or parole, and if yes, when does it expire?	0	1	2	3
Do they own their house or do they rent?	0	1	2	3
How clean do they keep their home?	0	1	2	3
Do you like the way they talk to you?	0	1	2	3
What is their religion and faith?	0	1	2	3

INFORMATION ITEMS	RATING STATEMENTS			
MONTHS **4-6** OF **DATING**	A. No bosom knowledge	B. Bosom knowledge that is not acceptable	C. Bosom knowledge that can be tolerated	D. Bosom knowledge that is accepted or not applicable
Where do they worship and how often, in which ministries are they active and what spiritual gifts do they recognize in themselves?	0	1	2	3
Are they saved and what do they understand to be the plan of salvation?	0	1	2	3
What is their purpose (i.e., goal, aim, desire, intention) in life?	0	1	2	3
Are they happy? If so, how does it show?	0	1	2	3
What is their mission (i.e., self-imposed duty or God-imposed will) in life?	0	1	2	3
What do they sense is the difference between God's voice and their personal desires and direction?	0	1	2	3
How many happily married friends do they have, and how many of them have been married at least ten years?	0	1	2	3

INFORMATION ITEMS	RATING STATEMENTS			
MONTHS **4-6** OF **DATING**	A. No bosom knowledge	B. Bosom knowledge that is not acceptable	C. Bosom knowledge that can be tolerated	D. Bosom knowledge that is accepted or not applicable
How many single people are in their family?	0	1	2	3
What are their views on abortion?	0	1	2	3
How do they feel about having half-siblings and step-siblings?	0	1	2	3
2. SUB-TOTAL FOR MONTHS 4-6 (20 items):	#:	#:	#:	#:
2. SUB-TOTAL SCORE: _____				

INFORMATION ITEMS	RATING STATEMENTS			
MONTHS **7-9** OF **DATING**	A. No bosom knowledge	B. Bosom knowledge that is not acceptable	C. Bosom knowledge that can be tolerated	D. Bosom knowledge that is accepted or not applicable
What is the person's birthday, place of birth and birth hospital? Were there any problems during their mother's pregnancy or delivery? Was the person adopted?	0	1	2	3
How often do they wash dishes, wash clothes, vacuum, dust, mop, etc. each week?	0	1	2	3

INFORMATION ITEMS	RATING STATEMENTS			
MONTHS 7-9 OF DATING	A. No bosom knowledge	B. Bosom knowledge that is not acceptable	C. Bosom knowledge that can be tolerated	D. Bosom knowledge that is accepted or not applicable
What type of housekeeper do people say they are?	0	1	2	3
Is the title to their automobile in their name?	0	1	2	3
Do they have a valid driver's license?	0	1	2	3
Do they have any outstanding tickets or warrants?	0	1	2	3
Have they ever been violent, abusive, or hit someone?	0	1	2	3
If yes, what happened? When was the first time? How frequently was it?	0	1	2	3
When was the last time it happened?	0	1	2	3
Have they shown signs of jealousy or control?	0	1	2	3
What licenses and certifications do they have?	0	1	2	3
What is the longest job they ever held?	0	1	2	3
How many jobs have they had in the past ten years?	0	1	2	3

INFORMATION ITEMS	RATING STATEMENTS			
MONTHS 7-9 OF **DATING**	A. No bosom knowledge	B. Bosom knowledge that is not acceptable	C. Bosom knowledge that can be tolerated	D. Bosom knowledge that is accepted or not applicable
What current problems are they experiencing with their job?	0	1	2	3
What barriers to gainful employment do they perceive that they have?	0	1	2	3
What positive employable factors do they possess?	0	1	2	3
Where do they work now?	0	1	2	3
What positions have they held for the past ten years?	0	1	2	3
Do they masturbate?	0	1	2	3
Have they undergone any gender/sex organ reassignment surgeries?	0	1	2	3
Are they HIV positive or do they have AIDS?	0	1	2	3
Do they plan on sharing their spouse with others sexually?	0	1	2	3
Are they comfortable with discussing sex?	0	1	2	3
Are they sexually active? If yes, what are their sexual activities?	0	1	2	3
Are they a virgin?	0	1	2	3

INFORMATION ITEMS	RATING STATEMENTS			
MONTHS 7-9 OF DATING	A. No bosom knowledge	B. Bosom knowledge that is not acceptable	C. Bosom knowledge that can be tolerated	D. Bosom knowledge that is accepted or not applicable
Have they ever engaged in homosexual, incestuous (sexual activity with family members), or pedophilic (sexual activity with children) activities—either as an adult or as a child?	0	1	2	3
What is their religious belief about premarital sex and sex within the bonds of marriage?	0	1	2	3
What is their political belief or association?	0	1	2	3
What is their ability to (1) keep promises, (2) be trustworthy, (3) admire, honor and respect their spouse, (4) enjoy the company of their spouse, (5) enjoy other's company with their spouse, (6) accept constructive criticism, (7) maintain a positive mood, and (8) consistently express rational and logical thoughts when they are at peace, upset or angry?	0	1	2	3
3. SUB-TOTAL FOR MONTHS 7-9 (30 items):	#:	#:	#:	#:
3. SUB-TOTAL SCORE: _____				

Information Items	Rating Statements			
Months 10-12 of **Dating**	A. No bosom knowledge	B. Bosom knowledge that is not acceptable	C. Bosom knowledge that can be tolerated	D. Bosom knowledge that is accepted or not applicable
How much to they read and what do they read?	0	1	2	3
Who raised the person?	0	1	2	3
Where were they raised?	0	1	2	3
What were the sleeping arrangements?	0	1	2	3
Who has had the strongest influence on their life?	0	1	2	3
What traumas have they experienced in life and how has it impacted them?	0	1	2	3
How much are they influenced by their family members and friends?	0	1	2	3
Who would the person describe their childhood?	0	1	2	3
Were they abused in any way (i.e.; emotional, mental, physical, sexual, etc.) as a child?	0	1	2	3
Were they neglected or abandoned as a child?	0	1	2	3

INFORMATION ITEMS	RATING STATEMENTS			
MONTHS **10-12** OF **DATING**	A. No bosom knowledge	B. Bosom knowledge that is not acceptable	C. Bosom knowledge that can be tolerated	D. Bosom knowledge that is accepted or not applicable
How often do they see their biological/adopted/foster children through the week, weekends, major holidays, minor holidays?	0	1	2	3
How do they feel about having more children?	0	1	2	3
How do they feel about adopting children?	0	1	2	3
How do they feel about having foster children?	0	1	2	3
How do they feel about having stepchildren?	0	1	2	3
Are they a party to active/outstanding paternity court actions?	0	1	2	3
Do they have any children or possible paternity court actions that could be brought against them?	0	1	2	3
If yes, what are the details about the children and/or possible paternity court actions?	0	1	2	3

INFORMATION ITEMS	RATING STATEMENTS			
MONTHS **10-12** OF **DATING**	A. No bosom knowledge	B. Bosom knowledge that is not acceptable	C. Bosom knowledge that can be tolerated	D. Bosom knowledge that is accepted or not applicable
What is their competency and ability to (1) solve ownership problems, (2) be a reliable source of information, (3) communicate clearly, (4) deal with emergencies, (5) be assertive, (6) argue constructively, (7) help solve a school subject problem with a child, (8) help with everyday medical problems, (9) help a child deal with a bully and (10) show leadership skills?	0	1	2	3
Emotionally, how do they reconcile with what people "say" they will do versus what people "actually do" when both behaviors are inconsistent?	0	1	2	3
How would they ensure that there would be consistent nonsexual romance in the marriage for an estimated 50-70 years?	0	1	2	3
What type of nonsexual romantic activity would they expect of you?	0	1	2	3

INFORMATION ITEMS	RATING STATEMENTS			
MONTHS 10-12 OF DATING	**A. No bosom knowledge**	**B. Bosom knowledge that is not acceptable**	**C. Bosom knowledge that can be tolerated**	**D. Bosom knowledge that is accepted or not applicable**
What type of nonsexual romance activities would they do for you as their spouse?	0	1	2	3
How easily do they forgive others for their transgressions?	0	1	2	3
How easily do they confess their sins, repent, and express remorse when they are wrong?	0	1	2	3
Do they foresee that they will need to assume responsibility for the care of a family member in the future (e.g., parents)?	0	1	2	3
What would be the daily/regular care options for the family member in need?	0	1	2	3
How many divorces have occurred in their family?	0	1	2	3
What is the infidelity history of their parents?	0	1	2	3
How many couples in their family are still married after 25 years?	0	1	2	3

INFORMATION ITEMS	RATING STATEMENTS			
MONTHS **10-12** OF **DATING**	A. No bosom knowl-edge	B. Bosom knowl-edge that is not accept-able	C. Bosom knowl-edge that can be tolerated	D. Bosom knowledge that is accepted or not applicable
Are these couples in their family happy? If so, how does it show?	0	1	2	3
Were either of their parents unfaithful (if applicable)?	0	1	2	3
What is the person's spirit, quality of thoughts, mood, emotional state, tone of voice, facial expression and interaction when they're happy, sad, stressed, or feeling indifferent?	0	1	2	3
4. SUB-TOTAL FOR MONTHS 10-12 (33 items):	#:	#:	#:	#:

4. SUB-TOTAL SCORE: _____

INFORMATION ITEMS	RATING STATEMENTS			
MONTHS **13-15** OF **DATING**	A. No bosom knowl-edge	B. Bosom knowl-edge that is not accept-able	C. Bosom knowl-edge that can be tolerated	D. Bosom knowledge that is accepted or not applicable
What medications have they taken or do they take now, and why?	0	1	2	3

INFORMATION ITEMS	RATING STATEMENTS			
MONTHS **13-15** OF **DATING**	**A. No bosom knowledge**	**B. Bosom knowledge that is not acceptable**	**C. Bosom knowledge that can be tolerated**	**D. Bosom knowledge that is accepted or not applicable**
What anti-psychotic or anti-depressant medication are they taking now?	0	1	2	3
What are the side effects of each medication?	0	1	2	3
Are they in compliance with their medication regime?	0	1	2	3
Is another person's name on their financial assets and/or debts, real property or personal property?	0	1	2	3
What is their debt status?	0	1	2	3
To whom do they owe money?	0	1	2	3
How much to each collector?	0	1	2	3
What debts are past due?	0	1	2	3
What is their debt elimination plan?	0	1	2	3
Have they ever been sued by a collector or filed for bankruptcy? If so, what was the outcome?	0	1	2	3
How much do they owe in child support/child care in arrears?	0	1	2	3

INFORMATION ITEMS	RATING STATEMENTS			
MONTHS **13-15** OF **DATING**	A. No bosom knowledge	B. Bosom knowledge that is not acceptable	C. Bosom knowledge that can be tolerated	D. Bosom knowledge that is accepted or not applicable
How much are they currently legally obligated to pay in child support/child care?	0	1	2	3
How do they distribute their net each payday?	0	1	2	3
What treatment have they receive at hospitals, medical clinics, substance abuse treatment programs, Narcotics Anonymous, Alcoholics Anonymous, or by psychiatrists, psychologists, psychiatric social workers or mental health professionals? When and why were they treated?	0	1	2	3
Do they wear any prostheses or artificial devices?	0	1	2	3
What are their vocational and socioeconomic dreams?	0	1	2	3
What are their goals for the next five to ten years?	0	1	2	3
What do they consider the difference between dreams and goals?	0	1	2	3

INFORMATION ITEMS	RATING STATEMENTS			
MONTHS **13-15** OF **DATING**	A. No bosom knowl-edge	B. Bosom knowl-edge that is not accept-able	C. Bosom knowl-edge that can be tolerated	D. Bosom knowledge that is accepted or not applicable
How much do they watch sports, soap operas and weekly programs on television?	0	1	2	3
How often do they gamble, travel, sleep each day, play golf, go shopping, or visit friends and relatives?	0	1	2	3
What sexual fantasies do they have?	0	1	2	3
If known, what do they believe would be their sexual/lovemaking pattern/program?	0	1	2	3
If known, what specific sexual acts (e.g., oral sex) do they expect to practice in marriage?	0	1	2	3
What are their views on birth control during the marriage?	0	1	2	3
What is the least number of days per week they would expect to have sexual intercourse with their spouse?	0	1	2	3
5. SUB-TOTAL FOR MONTHS 13-15 (25 items):	#:	#:	#:	#:
5. SUB-TOTAL SCORE: _____				

INFORMATION ITEMS	RATING STATEMENTS			
MONTHS **16-18** OF **DATING**	A. No bosom knowledge	B. Bosom knowledge that is not acceptable	C. Bosom knowledge that can be tolerated	D. Bosom knowledge that is accepted or not applicable
What is the person's financial status?	0	1	2	3
What savings accounts, checking accounts, IRAs, CDs, stocks, bonds, mutual funds, pensions, and other investments do they have?	0	1	2	3
How much do they have in each account?	0	1	2	3
When can copies of individual TRW, credit records, high school and college transcripts, tax returns (for the past three years), judgments of divorce, paternity orders, bankruptcy orders, resumes, signing of Pre-Nuptial agreements, criminal/civic/clearances/Last Will and Testaments, and bank/ investment statements for the past six months be exchanged?	0	1	2	3
What is their long-term financial plan?	0	1	2	3
How do they feel about the distribution of their wealth before and after their death?	0	1	2	3

INFORMATION ITEMS	RATING STATEMENTS			
MONTHS **16-18** OF **DATING**	A. No bosom knowledge	B. Bosom knowledge that is not acceptable	C. Bosom knowledge that can be tolerated	D. Bosom knowledge that is accepted or not applicable
How would they want to prepare their Last Will and Testament to allow for yourself, stepchildren, biological children, minor/adult children, organizations, siblings, extended relatives, friends, parents, etc.?	0	1	2	3
How do they feel about life support systems, transplants, and surgery?	0	1	2	3
What was the style of discipline used toward them when they were young?	0	1	2	3
Who disciplined them?	0	1	2	3
How did the person feel about the way they were disciplined?	0	1	2	3
What are their thoughts about how they would discipline their own children?	0	1	2	3

INFORMATION ITEMS	RATING STATEMENTS			
MONTHS 16-18 OF **DATING**	A. No bosom knowl-edge	B. Bosom knowl-edge that is not accept-able	C. Bosom knowl-edge that can be tolerated	D. Bosom knowledge that is accepted or not applicable
What is the overall potential or ability to (1) help a child deal with new situations, (2) help a child calm down, (3) recognize a child's need, (4) produce feelings of security for a spouse and children, (5) help children cope with fears, (6) create feelings of confidence for those in the family home, (7) be a patient listener, (8) be a reliable source of love, and (9) aid and assist your family and their own family?	0	1	2	3
Overall, how well would they consistently follow through with (1) enforcing homework assignments with children, (2) setting bedtime limits, (3) doing household chores, (4) paying household bills in a timely manner, (5) paying city, state and federal income taxes on time, (6) securing automobile license tabs on time, and (7) renewing their driver's license?	0	1	2	3

INFORMATION ITEMS	RATING STATEMENTS			
MONTHS **16-18** OF **DATING**	**A. No bosom knowledge**	**B. Bosom knowledge that is not acceptable**	**C. Bosom knowledge that can be tolerated**	**D. Bosom knowledge that is accepted or not applicable**
Overall, what were the main problems in their home when they were age Birth-1 years old, 4-5 years old, 6-11 years old, 12-20 years old, 20-24 years old, and 25-65 years old, and older?	0	1	2	3
In their family home, who was generally responsible for cooking, cleaning, writing the checks to pay bills, disciplining the children? Do they believe the distribution of responsibilities was effective and right?	0	1	2	3
6. SUB-TOTAL FOR MONTHS 16-18 (16 items):	#:	#:	#:	#:
6. SUB-TOTAL SCORE: _____				

TRANSFER OF SUM SUB-TOTALS:

SECTION 1 = _____   SECTION 5 = _____

SECTION 2 = _____   SECTION 6 = _____

SECTION 3 = _____

SECTION 4 = _____   **FDAA Total =** _____

INTERPRETING YOUR FDAA SCORE

The ultimate actualization score is 480 points. Because the Pre-Marital Screening Questionnaire (PMSQ) is a self-assessment test, the score is reliable only if there is honesty and a full, complete exchange of information between the dating parties. Low Full Disclosure and Acceptance (FDAA) scores are indicative of mere Pleasure Dating. High FDAA scores may indicate effective Investment Dating, or they could indicate a tendency to view the dating partner more favorably than is warranted—putting them in an unrealistically positive light. A high FDAA score, due to a pattern of excessive "not applicable" ratings, may reflect a failure to believe or accept the premise that full and honest discovery during courtship and dating can reduce the degree of marital discord, frustration, anger, bitterness and bewilderment often experienced after marriage. High FDAA Scores also could be the product of giving the maximum rating (i.e., a 3) on items that are partially known instead of fully known.

INTERPRETATION GUIDELINES

These are typical scores for those who are engaged in Investment and Biblical Dating, and it would appear that discussions about becoming engaged to enter into the covenant of marriage are appropriate after dating 12-18 months.

Total Score: 450 - 360

These are typical scores for those who are engaged in Investment Dating, but premarital or couple counseling is recommended to address individual differences before discussions about engagement or marriage should occur.

Total Score: 359-239

These are average scores for those engaged in mere Pleasure Dating. It would appear that gathering more information and bosom knowledge of the person is needed before any discussions about engagement or marriage should occur.

**Total Score:
240-120**

These are very low scores and the parties are merely engaged in Pleasure Dating and appear to be avoiding all unpleasant discussions about their personal and family histories.

**Total Score:
119-0**

Notes: _____

_____

_____

_____

_____

_____

_____

_____

_____

A person who is still looking good after the investigative dating period (typically, another four to six months) then becomes a candidate for "Investment Dating," the period in which two people begin to invest significant and exclusive time to determine whether they agree to put each other in the "Winner's Circle" of marriage.

Handling Unequal Premarital Assets and Wealth: CADES

In our present society, females are often becoming the major income earner in a significant number of American homes. If not handled well, this new phenomenon could be a detriment to the possible development of a wonderful and nourishing romantic relationship. To give guidance in this area, we recommend that each person follow our CADES principles:

C = Control and turf issues need to be resolved between both of you before the marital engagement.

A = Agreement about expenditures must be established and continuously discussed and resolved.

D = Disclosure about each parties' assets and debts must occur before the engagement and then continuously.

E = Egos must be kept under control. Male's *egos* are usually attached to money, and most female's sense of *security* is attached to money.

S = Sensitivity about each parties' financial needs and wants must be respected. Both persons must assume responsibility for articulating all of their reasonable financial needs and the other partner must lovingly want to meet that need. Thus, both parties must be each other's "help meet."

Be wise and remember that it is best to establish joint bank accounts only if there can be a significant cushion of money placed in each account. The person who has been the most financially responsible, with the best daily time management and communication skills, should have the primary responsibility for assuring that the household bills are paid and handling the marital finances. Regardless of the lack of parity among the individual pots of monies, each person in the relationship must respect each other and feel that they are comrades and financial partners together in a joint venture. Both romantic partners must learn how to have some "fun money" (i.e. vacations, dining out, concerts, etc.), and each person must be in control of some flow of the money (e.g. the person who pays the household bills receives 85% of the joint pots of money and the remaining 15% is shared by both parties). Partners should not choose a non-momentary flow position. After they get married, each party must stay abreast and knowledgeable about the status of the family debts, assets and financial distribution. Know what you know!

WISDOM BOX #8:

1. You must have "bosom knowledge," tolerance and acceptance of every trait and aspect of your romantic partner.

2. Your romantic partner's behavior that is merely tolerated today may lead to anger, hurt, frustration and fear tomorrow.

3. Gender should not dictate who should handle the marital finances.

4. Whoever has the most (a) financial responsibility, (b) punctuality with time management, (c) communication skill, and (d) negotiation skill should be responsible for paying the household bills and managing the marital finances.

Chapter Ten

Preparation for Marriage

When you chase God, the godly and holy man or woman will chase you. If you want romance with another, improve your intimacy with God. Psalm 37 tells us "Delight thyself also in the Lord and he shall give thee the desires of thine heart. Commit thy way unto the Lord; trust also in him and he shall bring it to pass."

When dating you can't be like the bridesmaids in Matthews 25:6, who failed to keep their lamps lit in preparation for the coming of the bridegroom. We have to do our part to get our spirit and life prepared for marriage. To get prepared for marriage, we need to stop the train of self destruction and take an airplane to our ultimate destination in Jesus Christ. Romans 8:38-39 and Habakkuk 3:7-19 tell us although the manifestations of our prayers are not seen, we can gain our strength from the Lord and He shall make us walk high. Walk in the direction of your belief and faith. Believe that there is someone for you, but be cautious and steady in your investigation. Exodus 13:17-18 demonstrates that sometimes it's best to go the long route instead of taking the shortcut. Enjoy the journey of singleness; nothing shall separate you from the love of God, because healthy holy single people are separate, unique, different and whole. Allow your Father God to guide you beyond your hopes and dreams.

The waiting period for a spouse should be a meaningful time spent not only in preparation, but also in enjoying the journey and/or the pursuit of a suitable spouse, if so desired. Social dating and investigative dating are fun and informative ways to spend this waiting period.

While you are waiting and preparing for marriage, don't waddle in depression and self pity. Instead, use this time to improve your "Romantic Market Value (RMV)" as coined by Dr. Larry E. Davis (1993). Use this time for self-improvement projects, such as:

- Body image and weight
- Tone of voice
- Personality
- Self-esteem
- Emotional intelligence
- Self-affirmation
- Interpersonal communication skills
- Social skills
- Recreation skills
- Professional status
- Annual income
- Education
- Social status
- Spirituality
- Financial credit status
- Home environment
- Transportation
- Attractiveness

While waiting for "Mr. or Ms. Right" to arrive, don't forget to participate in social, recreational, cultural, and political events. To be interesting to someone, you have to have interests; you have to have things to talk about. These kinds of activities help!

How to Pray for the Desires of Your Heart

"Delight yourself in the Lord, and He will give you the desires of your heart." (Psalm 37:4) We can't say that enough. But for prayer to be effective, you must first:

- prepare your heart, mind and spirit by focusing on God.
- ask God to forgive you for any specific wrongdoing toward others, including your former spouse if you've been married before.
- if possible, pray with your intended partner, out loud and holding hands; as well as individually for one another.

When you pray, ask for:

- faith, favor, grace, mercy and strength.
- protection from hurt, harm and dangers in the environment and world.

As often as possible each person in a romantic relationship should choose a particular place in their private residential space to pray for each other. This pray place should include a Bible, books, and reading material on various subjects. It is important to use this pray place for prayer and worship only, and not physical intimacy. Try the kitchen table, family room, etc.

Prayer is not just communication with God. It is being with God (Graf, 2002). Singles, has your prayer been for a specific man or woman in the flesh, or has your prayer been righteous and holy like the one leper in Luke 17:13? The leper could have been very specific and lifted his voice and cried "Jesus, Master, heal me from my skin disease," with a compulsive Martha type of spirit. Martha, the one who busied herself instead of sitting at the feet of Jesus. But instead the leper only said "Jesus, Master have mercy on us," with a Mary type of spirit. Mary, the one who sat at His feet and delighted herself in his presence, knowing that was the better thing.

Open your prayers up so that your prayers humble you and usher you into the presence of God, so that God can bless you as he desires. It is best to learn find the "inner core eye" of your spirit where the Holy Spirit dwells within you. Some of your prayers can be specific; but you should also learn how to pray a "seeking" prayer—one that doesn't ask for something from God's hand, but instead seeks His face:

> *"Dear Lord, I humble myself before you with thanksgiving in my heart. Thank you for the awesome blessings that have flowed from heaven. Thank you for loving me and giving us your son Jesus Christ. I confess my sins and transgressions. I have a repentance spirit and remorseful heart and now ask for your forgiveness, and strength to live better tomorrow. Lord I am lonely and desire a companion that I can share my blessed life with. Lord, you know that I love you and that you are my Lord and Savior. Lord, you know your child here and you know the man/woman that I need. Please Lord, usher them into my life now and give me the wisdom and discernment to recognize him/her and to gain their favor. I trust you Lord, and my spirit is open to your blessing in my life. Please continue to prepare and anoint my spouse and release them to me in due season. Lord strengthen me and continue to develop me to be the wife/husband that you need for me to be in the kingdom. In Jesus name I pray. Amen and Hallelujah."*

WISDOM BOX #9:

1. When you chase God, the godly and holy man or woman will chase you.

2. While you are waiting, don't waddle in depression and self pity, but instead improve your "Romantic Market Value."

Chapter Eleven

The Empowerment of Unrevealed Miracles in an Engaging and Determined Single Life

Living by a mature faith brings self-empowerment and rich possibilities. We are saved and then we begin our walk of faith. Roman 5:16 tells us that faith is the key and we are certain to receive it if we have faith like Abraham who is the father of all who believe. Mature faith is:

1. believing that the same God that has given you victories in the past is the same God that has the power to do whatever you need him to do now.

2. believing that God is able to do what he wants to do in each of your lives.

3. believing that you must bow to the sovereign God.

4. believing that there are some things you must be settled about—if He is keeping you then there is something He has in store to bless you with.

Living in the revelation of intimate knowledge and hopeful expectation brings self-empowerment. Ephesians 1:18 tells us to pray that our hearts will be flooded with light so that we can understand the wonderful future that God has promised to those he has called.

God is standing ready to pour great things into the lives of those who believe and trust Him. God is here right now ready to pour great blessings into your life because He loves you and He thinks you are worthy of His many awesome blessings.

137

PERSONAL TESTIMONY:

It was the final semester of high school, and by the grace of God my name was on the graduation list. Aunt Bernice asked me what my plans were. I told her that I wanted to get married. She held her peace, and with the settled peace and in the spirit of Naomi, she said, "Baby, is there anyone in your life who you plan to marry at this time?" I gave it some thought and said, "No Ma'am." She was able to breathe again. Aunt Bernice said, "Well, since you don't have a candidate for marriage at this time, why don't you go to college and get your Bachelor's degree?" I said, "OK." With the help of Aunt Bernice, Uncle Jerry, my mother and a host of uncles, aunts and cousins, I proceeded to achieve that goal. Life ensued. At the graduation ceremony for receiving my Bachelor of Arts Degree, Aunt Bernice prayed first and then asked me, "Baby, what do you want to do now?" I answered, "I want to get married." Aunt Bernice prayed first, composed herself and said, "Baby, is there anyone in your life who you plan to marry at this time?" I said, "No Ma'am." She thanked the Lord and said, "Well since you don't have a candidate for marriage at this time, why don't you go to graduate school and get your Master's degree? I said, "OK." With more difficulties, life proceeded on. At the graduation ceremony for my Master of Education Degree, Aunt Bernice called on the name of our Lord and Savior Jesus Christ, and asked me, "Baby, what do you want to do now?" I answered, "I want to get married." Aunt Bernice tapped into the Holy Spirit inside her and said, "Baby, is there anyone in your life who you plan to marry at this time?" I said, "No Ma'am." She thanked her Father God and said, "Well since you don't have a candidate for marriage at this time, why don't you go to graduate school and get your Doctorate degree?" I said "OK." I was always an obedient and respectful child. And life happened anyway. Instead of wasting time by being unproductive, waddling in my self pity and depression about not having a candidate for marriage I improved my romantic market value. Robert and I knew each other professionally for 15 years before we actually saw each other. And we only saw each other after Robert separated from his wife and we both rededicated our-

selves to God. We only saw each other after Rob was celibate for five years and I was celibate for nine months. Our celibacy represented two other unrevealed miracles of God.

When I took my eyes off of getting married, then my husband came. The lesson that I learned by submitting to my shepherd God and being obedient to my wise elder was that the miracle I was looking for was not the miracle that I received. I was wanting and looking for a husband but I received a full education. I was wanting and looking for a husband, but I received provision from two occupations. I was wanting a husband, but I received a ministry of Christian counseling, and that ministry placed me in a position to seek first the kingdom of God and his righteousness by providing Christian counseling services to others. And it was through providing Christian counseling and mental health services that I met my beloved husband, Robert Dee Williams. The miracle I was looking for was not the miracle that I received.

We must have a "made-up mind" to practice the simple childlike obedience of faith and totally yield our will to the written word of God. The New Living Translation of Ephesians 5:15-20 reads, "So be careful how you live, not as fools but as those who are wise, make the most of every opportunity for doing good in these evil days. Don't act thoughtlessly, but try to understand what the Lord wants you to do. Don't be drunk with sex, lust and wine, because that will ruin your life. Instead, let the Spirit fill and control you."

Throughout your day, sing psalms, hymns and spiritual songs which will make joyful and quite worship to the Lord in your hearts. We can eliminate unhealthy emotions and become empowered when we speak the name of Jesus out loud and when we hum a song that encourages ourselves and positively speaks to our spirit. Make Donnie McClurkin's song "I'll Trust You Lord" your mantra and those words can radiant in your spirit during challenging times. What song of hope and faith does your spirit sing as you walk through life each day? You need to allow uplifting spiritual songs to minister to your spirit and bring you peace.

When we align ourselves with the scriptures we can learn how to discriminate the difference between the voice of God and the voice of our inner fleshly self. Your purpose in life should come forth out of your natural spiritual and ministerial gifts. Ask the Holy Spirit to reveal to you what is your purpose in life and let that drive you. *Your purpose in life is not to marry.* Remember that Adam did not ask for a wife. Genesis 3:22 tells us that God "made he a woman, and brought her into the man Adam."

We need to feel a Jeremiah-like purpose in our life—we need to have a sense of personal engagement power. God can take something insufficient like Moses and the burning bush and set it on fire and let it become the vehicle through with something important can flow. If the power of God gets in you then you can become powerful. With the power of God on your life, you can talk like Jesus instead of talking like those unhealthy persons that may have raised you or like those wrongdoers that have negatively influenced you.

We need to get on fire for some sort of work in the kingdom of God. Through prayer and quiet mediation you can know your purpose in life—your spiritual gifts and how God has anointed your life.

Remember that with God, all things are possible, even if your single life and home environment has been harsh, drought-stricken, dormant, destroyed, rocky or dead. Come what may you can seek from God hope, faith, a peaceful spirit, discernment and wisdom. He will help you become a new creature in Christ with the personal power needed for your beautiful single life to flourish.

You are a beautiful saved vessel placed high up in a holy place. We want to tell you that God loves you, He is faithful to His Word and He gives you new mercies each morning. Forgive yourself for yesterday and trust the Lord. Come what may you have the power of great expectation. Remember that the devil has to confront you with your past and your personal weaknesses because he has no control over your future. God has a promise you should hold on to and look forward to. Come what may, just step out, be happy, live, and trust the Lord.

Our future is in our mind and our spirit. Our future is determined by how we manage our circumstances. Our spirit determines how we respond, react, cope with and handle victories, defeats and life-changing events. Our spirit is like an energy force. Our spirit determines our attitude. And to prevent an ungodly spirit or attitude we must do what Timothy did in Second Timothy 2:22: "Run from anything that stimulates our youthful lust." That takes concentrating on God; it is only then that the Word of God can work in your life.

Follow anything that makes you want to do right. God will know your integrity by how balanced your life is. Singles need to be "lifestyle setters," not "style setters." Singles must be steadfast to a Christian moral code that communicates their integrity and accountability to their faith and to others. Pursue faith, love, peace, and enjoy the companionship of those who call on the Lord with pure hearts.

Our companionship with God and our companionships with others mold our spirit and our attitude. Be mindful as to who you have in your thoughts and your mind. Those who walk through your thoughts determine your image of yourself.

Create a rich life that is full of activities that you can control. Don't create a life that is depended on the choices and behaviors of others. Note the box of life in Figure 1. The box of life is full, but it is

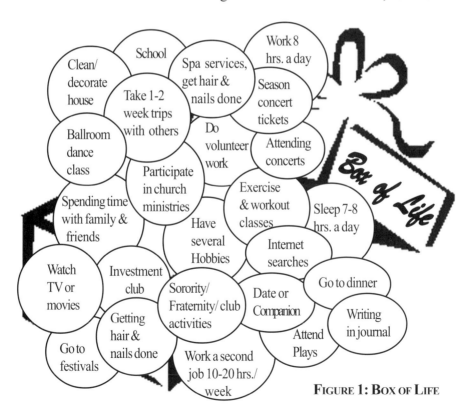

FIGURE 1: BOX OF LIFE

full of self-directed activities. The box of life is not full of activities that require a romantic partner. In relationship to the overall picture, the presence of the romantic partner is insufficient without the other aspects. Remember that your world should not be centered around a love interest. Explore other activities and expand the boundaries of your life. Women, remember that men are competitive and tend to be attracted to what is not easily attainable. Women, it is best to appear unavailable if you want to gain the attention of a man. Men remember that women see relationships as their first priority; they are socially aware and respond to romance. It is best to have a full and vibrant life that she can participate in along with you.

In our "Box of Life" we created a vision of a full and happy holy single lifestyle. It is crucial that you have a vision of your life that is full of diversity, spiritual rewards, and gratification. Fill your life with activities and meaningful actions that give you a sense of engagement and fulfillment. Claim the moment, be happy and be blessed.

I Corinthians 7:32-34 tells us that "he that is unmarried careth for the things that belong to the Lord, how he may please the Lord...The unmarried woman careth for the things of the Lord, that she may be holy both in body and in spirit; but that married careth for the things of the world, how she may please her husband." Righteous is knowing and doing what the Bible says. Holiness is to set yourself apart from the world and behave in a way that is consistent with what you know that the Bible directs you to do. Let the Word of God and our testimonies empower you, engage you and encourage you to move toward your purpose in life.

WISDOM BOX #10:

1. When you stop being preoccupied with getting married, seek productive activities to fulfill your God-given purpose in life, then your God-given husband or wife will arrive.

2. Our future is determined by how we control our circumstances.

Chapter Twelve

Stewardship

If we are grateful to God for what He has given to us through His grace then we should marshal our blessings. If we are appreciative for our real estate and personal property then we should be a good steward over all of our belongings within the kingdom of God. To be a good steward, we must carefully manage our Christian household. There are three different camps of thought that we would encourage you to consider before the period of engagement.

Trust…but Verify

Regardless of the lies we tell ourselves, love really is conditional. Love is conditional on the truth. And an omission can constitute a lie. Reportedly, former President Ronald Reagan's political stance toward the Soviet Union was "Trust…but verify." We take this same posture in romantic relationships. Prior to engagement and marriage, and/or making a significant financial investment in a romantic partner, it is our professional opinion that both parties should *verify* all material personal information that has been received. Yes, the coauthors of this book also completed the same verification process six months before the announcement of their engagement. We dated for three and a half years before our period of engagement.

The New Living Translation commentary for Luke 16:1-8 instructs us that:

Our use of money is a good test of the lordship of Christ. (1) Let us use our resources wisely because they belong to God, and not to us, (2) Money can be used for good or evil; let us use ours for good, (3) Money has a lot of power, so we must use it carefully and thoughtfully, (4) We must use our material goods in a way that will foster faith and obedience.

In harmony with those opinions, we strongly advise that you complete a comprehensive verification search of a romantic partner prior to the engagement period that researches the following:

- Adoption Records
- Birth Records
- Ancestry.com
- Asset Research
- Assumed Names County Clerk Registration
- Bankruptcies
- Circuit Court and Probate Court Case Record System
- Civil Court Record & Judgments
- Corporate Affiliations
- County Clerk Marriage License Bureau
- County Criminal Records Check
- County Register of Deeds
- Grant and Grantee Search
- Credit Bureau Checks (all three companies)
- Criminal Offenders
- District County Court Small Claims System
- Divorce Records
- Driver License Records Information
- Driver Record

- Education Verification
- E-mail Address Finding
- Employment Verification
- Federal Bankruptcy Lien System
- FEIN
- Google.com
- How To Investigate.com
- Marriage License Records
- Military Locator and Records
- Motor Vehicles Registration
- National Death Index
- Nationwide Criminal Records
- Nationwide Property Ownership
- Occupational License Verification
- Platinum–detective.com
- P.O. Box Trace
- Sexual Offender Search
- Social Security Number Check
- State Criminal Records Check
- State Department of Corrections On-line Offender Name Search
- State Professional Licensing Internet Search
- Tax Lien System
- Voters Registration

Before the engagement we strongly advise each of you to discuss and achieve mutual agreement and decide on the terms, bequeaths and distribution of real and personal property relative to your intended spouse, prior biological children, stepchildren, parents, relatives, and future children of your possible union. Then the Last Will and Testament should be revoked, and a codicil, or a new document should be drafted after receiving competent legal consultation. There are far too many mature widows, widowers, and divorcees who re-marry, but leave this matter unattended, and in time, this issue has caused people to separate and/or divorce. The matter of your estate will not resolve itself as a product of time, love, or a verbal commitment by your romantic partner to take care of your prior children, parents and family.

Third, if either of you have significant real and/or personal property, privately owned corporations, family businesses, pending lawsuits, and/or possible substantial inheritance, then receive legal advice and counsel whether you should consider a Premarital Agreement (also known as Separation, Antenuptial or Prenuptial Agreements). Each party should be mindful of their rights, liabilities, property affairs, financial affairs, prior marital alimony, claims, and any and all interests available to them in their jurisdiction.

Trust is like being putty dough in a romantic partner's hands. It is not wise to blindly trust who we do not know as well as "The Potter." Trust, but verify. God loves us so much and he has blessed us with many possessions and resources within the kingdom of God. Matthew 25:14-30 teaches us that God expects us to invest and maintain our resources wisely so that we can enable and further the work of the Kingdom. These methods of investigation and protection are merely designed to strengthen and support covenant marriages that are ordained and blessed by God, and ensure that they are not guided by the destructive hand of the evil one.

Preparing for Marital Servitude

In our society we often have a misguided sense of entitlement. Even as saved single Christians, we may take on the clothing of "diva-ness" and "playerism." Neither posture will survive singlehood and transform into a strong married lifestyle. True love and marital servitude means to be skillful in *"asking, hearing and then delivering"* what your spouse articulates are their desires, needs and wants. That is not the same as coming to our own conclusions as to what is in the best interest for our spouse and then meeting that need. To honor marital servitude requires one to respect the "self-proclaimed or elective silence" of our spouse. We should not consider our own deductive reasoning abilities to be superior to that of our spouse. When we sincerely attempt to satisfy the personal needs of our romantic partners and spouses, but our actions are not appreciated, we often become defensive and offended. You must view servitude to your intended spouse as a skill that you bring to the marriage and not view it as oppression. This tendency to see true marital servitude as slave-like oppression is a particular risk in the African American community, where our generational memories continue to haunt and distort. Press to free your mind.

But to serve your anticipated marriage, you must desire to meet the needs of your romantic partner or spouse from their perspective and not your own. Servants lean on God and not their own understanding. Servants count on God to be faithful even if their spouse is not. A commitment to serve the expressed needs of your spouse must be a priority to loving them. A commitment to being honor-bound to obey what your wife or husband articulates they want or need you to do is ministering to them. That is why it is important to only marry the person who you can make the commitment of marital servitude with, instead of marrying the person who you merely love. In God's eye love is a lifetime covenant—so what does love have to do with it? Serve her peacefully and devotedly or don't marry her. Serve him enthusiastically and quietly or don't marry him. Be prepared to serve. Be prepared to give and not receive. If both have that posture there will be parity. Transform your perception to see yourself entering into marriage in order to glorify and serve God through the marriage. View the marriage as a vehicle through which both of you can fulfill God's calling on your lives. Remember it's not about you changing your name, having companionship, having your physical needs met, having safe sex, or a set of warm arms around you. Everything you do should be about God, and to the glory of God. Now insert smile!

The Call to Singleness

It is a blessing to be single and perfectly fine to stay single. Matthew 6:17-24 charges us to have spiritual vision which is our capacity to see the world from God's point of view. But self-serving desires, interest and goals can block that version. Serving God is the best way to restore it. A pure eye is one that is fixed on God.

Some of us can see ourselves being successful as a wife or husband, but not successful as a single person. Others of us have a special singleness "call." A call to singleness has some specific characteristics; namely:

1. There is a clear message from the Holy Spirit that being free of any spousal encumbrances feels natural, peaceful and free to you.

2. Other Christians who have observed the fruit of your labor and those that have the gifts of discernment and exhortation affirm your call to singlehood.

3. As a direct result of functioning and laboring in your natural gifts from God, you see results that bring you such sweet fruits in the Kingdom of God, that the gratification you receive is more than enough to satisfy; and if you were married, it is obvious that such a service to others in the Kingdom of God would not be feasible.

    • Don't idolize marriage too much. The majority of you will be disappointed with the institution of marriage within the first three years. God didn't create you to be desperate; desperation creates depression and delusions.

Isaiah 54:5 tells us "For thy maker is thine husband; the Lord of hosts is his name; and thy Redeemer the Holy One of Israel; the God of the whole earth shall he be called." God may sacrifice your dignity in order to protect your God-given destiny. Often a chosen single person is called to make a sacrifice in order to fill a gap in the Kingdom because of their godly character. If what you are doing is what God told you to do then you must cope with and handle whatever comes. If what you are doing is what God told you to do, you must accept the circumstances that result from the calling. You must be strong enough to tell all potential romantic partners that your Christian principles are more important to you than enjoying the pleasure of their body. You need to separate what you know the Holy Spirit is telling you from the values expressed to you by others. If you are called to singlehood, celebrate it and grow deeper in your faith.

Only the creator of a product can tell you the true value of that product. God created you so He is the only one who can tell you your worth. He is the only one who can judge and evaluate you. We can have only one Master and whatever, or whoever you lean on and listen to will become your Master. Don't allow others to judge your singlehood. Obey your Master, Father God, and enjoy the beauty of your singlehood!

The Call to Marriage

Marriage is not a "Rites of Passage" to womanhood or manhood. Marriage is a calling from God. Marriage may be consistent with God's divine plan for your life. A call to marriage is a serious matter. A call to marriage is an inner urge, a strong directive to marry. It should be undertaken with much thoughtfulness. Persons seeking marriage should first consult with God to determine if this is truly an urge or a "call" or simply a personal human flesh desire to marry a partner for a multitude of reasons. You must be certain and knowledgeable of what marriage entails prior to making a sincere commitment to a partner. A call to marriage is independent and has nothing to do with the number of years you have invested in the relationship. For example, just because you have dated for four years doesn't mean that you have a call to marriage with that person. Just because you are getting older and your childbearing years are fading, doesn't mean that there is a call to marriage. Just because you are a male over 40 years old and living home with your mother doesn't mean you have a call to marriage. Genesis 2:21 tells us that Adam was exposed and Eve was created and then God restored him by closing him up. God brought Eve to Adam. Adam did not ask for or seek Eve.

A call to marriage requires consideration given to the other persons who are involved in your life, including children, parents, grandparents, godparents, siblings, childhood friends, extended family members and significant others. These persons are vital to the survival and success of a marriage because of what they contribute to the welfare of that marriage. The support of these persons is necessary initially and on an ongoing basis.

A call to marriage must be spirit filled in which God has anointed the chosen relationship. Following the call to marriage, Christian counseling is advised until the relationship is considered satisfactory and God-centered in nature.

PERSONAL TESTIMONY:

It was like undergoing plastic surgery, resurrection, make-over, and transformation. It was a life saving event. I was a log and Paris chiseled something beautiful. I was a piece of marble and Paris was my sculptor. I was a diamond in the rough and Paris applied a polish that made me shine before the world.

When we first met, Paris made it clear that she loved my mind, heart and spirit, but she couldn't accept my Don King hairstyle, my one gray pin-striped suit and missing back teeth. I was offended, embarrassed and defensive. The challenge she presented to me was to improve those areas of my life or lose her telephone number. There was something about her blunt honesty that caused me to trust her and have faith in her counsel and advice.

After soaking my ego for two weeks I called her and told her that I needed her help. Paris took me to her hair stylist friend who cut, relaxed and tamed my hair. On my next pay day Paris took me to her favorite men's clothing store, introduced me to her favorite salesman, and supervised my selecting two suits, along with matching shirts, ties, shoes, cuff-links and tie clips. Paris took me to her Uncle Jerry who is a dentist in order to be fitted for a partial denture. On September 17th we had our first date. I arrived at her home with my new hair style, new outfit, replacement teeth, and fresh-cut roses. Even I knew I looked good. Paris opened the door, saw me and for the first time she was speechless. Paris then declared "That's it—no one is going to be with you except me—no one is going to get you now." I blushed. And after that day, no one every did get my attention but Paris. I love her for caring for me and guiding me to the transformed self that I envisioned. God intended for me to be her diamond in the rough.

If you don't like the behavior you see with your eyes then do not marry. Do you know your diamond in the rough only requires a little polish in order to be a blessing to your life? After you have married, it is important to accept your decision to marry that specific person, staying focused on what is good in the partner instead of what is lacking. To be in step with your call to marriage you must be able to release the ill feelings, disappointment and anger with yourself for marrying someone who does not fit the image of the mate you dreamed about nor who meets your every expectation for a spouse. If your call to marriage was not what you expected, then get over it and enjoy the true marriage set before you. Pray for change, peacefully establish mutual agreements toward change, and always be content in the moment.

Learn to love the one you consciously chose to marry. Fully accept your own free-will decision to marry a person whom you are not pleased with. Learn how to forgive yourself for making unwise decisions. This higher level of consciousness will make it easier to achieve marital contentment and see your spouse as your refuge and as your home.

Know that each of you is empowered to establish healthy romantic and marital relationships. Know that the same power that is in God is already in you. And your God given power has bestowed in you certain rights, privileges and authority (Matthew 28:18). Be empowered and responsible for your happiness; God has given you the spirit of power, and of love, and of a sound mind! Know that you are queens and kings. "Ye are a chosen generation, a royal priesthood, an holy nation, a peculiar people" (I Peter 2:9a). Be Sister Queens and Brother Kings. Look up, cheer up, be happy, live well and responsibly, and be blessed.

WISDOM BOX #11:

1. Trust but verify important information disclosed or relative to your romantic partner.

2. Only marry a person that you can serve.

3. Polish the diamond in the rough that God has planted in your path in this life *before* you get engaged.

Appendix

Resources and References

The *Abolition of Marriage* by Maggie Gallagher page 117, Dennis A. Ahlburg and Carol J. DeVita, *"New Realities of the American Family,"* Population Bulletin 47, No. 2 (August 1992): 15.

Adams, Kimberly Rene. "African American Father-Daughter Relationships Across the Lifespan: *An Innovative Approach."* *Building on Family Strength Conference*, 1999, Cited on page 58.

Adams, Ty. *"Single, Saved and Having Sex."* Detroit, Michigan: Heaven Enterprises, 2003.

Ahlburg, first name, and first name DeVita. *New Realities*, 4-12. Cited on page 5 of *The Abolition of Marriag*e by Maggie Gallagher. City: Publisher, Date.

Barna Research Group. (No Date). *Divorce Rates in the U.S.* (Religious Tolerance). [On-line].
Available: http:// www.religioustolerance.org [February 8, 2005].

Barna Research Group. (No Date). (*Family*). [On-line].
Available: http://PageCategory.asp. [March 12, 2001]

Berman, Jennifer. (No Date). *FAQs on Female Sexual Dysfunction* [On-line]. Available: http://www.msnbc.com/news. [July 11, 2000].

Black, Sabrina D., *Can Two Walk Together?* Chicago, Illinois: Moody Press, 2002.

Blankehorn, David, Steve Bayme, and Jean Bethke. *Rebuilding the Nest: A New Commitment to the American Family,* ed. (Milwaukee, WI: Family Service America, c. 1990), 97-98. Cited on page 8 of *The Abolition of Marriage* by Maggie Gallagher.

Clinton, Dr. Tim. *Before a Bad Goodbye*: *How to Turn Your Marriage Around*. Nashville, TN: Word Publishing, 1999.

Clinton, Tim and Gary Sibcy. *Attachments.* Brentwood, TN, 2002.

Davis, Larry E. *Black and Single.* Chicago, Illinois: The Noble Press, Inc., 1993.

Farrel, Bill and Pam. *Single Men Are Like Waffles Single Women Are Like Spaghetti.* Eugene, Oregon, Harvest House Publishers, 2002.

Finner-Williams, Paris and Robert Williams, *Marital Secrets: Dating, Lies, Communication and Sex*, Detroit, Michigan: RP Publishing, 2005.

Graf, Jonathan, *The Power of Personal Prayer.* Colorado Springs, Colorado: Nava Press, 2002.

Hammond, Michelle McKinney. *What To Do Until Love Finds You.* Eugene, Oregon, Harvest House Publishers, 1997.

Hart, Archibald D. *The Hart Report: The Sexual Man.* Grand Rapids, MI: Zondervan Publishing House, 1994.

Jake, T.D., *The Potter's House Presents: 7 Steps To A Turn-Around.* T.D. Jake Ministries. Dallas, Texas, 2004.

Kozier, Barbara, and Glenora Lea Erb. *Fundamentals of Nursing: Concepts and Procedures.* Englewood Cliffs, NJ: Prentice-Hall, 1999.

Krejcir, Richard. (No Date). *"Blame Shifting"* [On-line]. Available: http://www.christianity.com/partner. [July 12, 2003].

Martin, Teresa Castro and Larry L. Bumpass. "Recent Trends in Marital Disruption." *Demography 26* (1989): 37-51. Cited on page 5 of *The Abolition of Marriage* by Maggie Gallagher.

Miller, William, R., *"Resolutions That Work," Spirituality & Health,* January/February, 2005, cited on page 46.

Nietzel, M.T. and D.A Bernstein. *Introduction to Clinical Psychology.* Citing Erick H. Erickson on page 38. Englewood Cliffs, NJ: Prentice-Hall, 1987.

Osaigbovo, Rebecca. *Chosen Vessels: Women of Color, Keys to Change.* Detroit, MI: DaBaR Services, 1992.

Osaigbovo, Rebecca. *It's Not About You: It's About God.* Downers, Grove, Illinois. InterVarsity Press, 2003.

Osaigbovo, Rebecca. *Movin' On Up: A Woman's Guide Beyond Religion to Spirit-Filled Living.* Detroit, MI: Dabar Publishing, 1997.

Reeder, Diane Proctor, *A Diary of Joseph: A Spiritual Journey Through Time.* Southfield, Michigan: Written Images, 2000.

Rosenblatt, Stanley, *The Divorce Racket.* City: Nash Publishing, 1969.

Taueg, Cynthia. *Faces of Faith.* Enumclaw, WA, Wine Press Publishing, 2004.

Taueg, Cynthia. *Planting Seeds For The Harvest of a Successful Marriage: A Guide For Women.* Lincoln Park, MI: To the Glory of God Ministries, Date.

Thurman, Chris. *The Lies We Believe.* Nashville, IN: Thomas Nelson Publishers, 1989.

Vernick, Leslie. *Getting Over The Blues.* Eugene, Oregon: Harvest

Index

Share with Others

Single Wisdom and Marital Secrets: Datings, Lies, Communication and Sex

Name: _____

Address: _____

City: _____ State: ____ Zip Code: _____

Day Telephone: (_____) _____

Order		Quantity	Price	
	Single Wisdom	_____	$17.95/book	
	Marital Secrets	_____	$15.95/book	
	Subtotal			
	Priority Shipping & Handling		$4.00/book	_____
	MI residents add 6% sales tax			_____
	Total			_____

Method of Payment

❑ Check or Money Order enclosed (make payable to RP Publishing)

❑ Visa ❑ Mastercard Acct. No.: _____

Exp. Date: _____ Signature: _____

Mail this form with payment to:

RP Publishing
17629 West McNichols Road
Detroit, MI 48235

For faster service:
Phone: 888.955.5055 or 313.537.1000
Fax: 313.537.0363
e-mail: finnerwilliams@aol.com

Order Online: www.Finner-Williams.com

These books are available at special quantity discounts for bulk purchases for sales promotions, fund-raising, or educational use. Special books or book excerpts can also be created to fit specific needs. Please contact us at 888.955.5055 regarding quantity discounts.

This offer is subject to change without notice.